ROYAL
SHAKESPEARE
COMPANY

SIR THOMAS MORE

ANTHONY MUNDAY
AND OTHERS

revised by

HENRY CHETTLE, THOMAS DEKKER
THOMAS HEYWOOD AND
WILLIAM SHAKESPEARE

NICK HERN BOOKS
LONDON
www.nickhernbooks.co.uk

Other NHB/RSC Titles

The Royal Shakespeare Company

The Royal Shakespeare Company is one of the world's best-known
theatre ensembles, and aims to create outstanding theatre relevant to
our times. The RSC is at the leading edge of classical theatre, with an
international reputation for artistic excellence, accessibility and high-
quality live performance.

Gunpowder is a season of explosive political drama to celebrate both the
four-hundredth anniversary of the Gunpowder Plot and the twentieth
anniversary of the Swan Theatre. The season of rare Elizabethan and
Jacobean plays includes a Shakespeare apocryphal play, a satirical black
comedy, and two political thrillers, finishing with a specially
commissioned new play.

Building on the success of both the first Jacobean Season in 2002 and
the Spanish Golden Age Season in 2004, the RSC is again presenting a
body of rarely performed work for a modern audience.

The RSC performs throughout the year at our home in Stratford-upon-
Avon and that work is complemented by a presence in other areas of the
UK. We play regularly in London and at an annual residency in Newcastle
upon Tyne. In addition, our mobile auditorium tour plays in community
centres, sports halls and schools in areas throughout the UK with little
access to professional theatre.

While the UK is the home of our Company, our audiences are global. We
regularly play to theatregoers in other parts of Europe, across the United
States, the Americas, Asia and Australasia and we are proud of our
relationships with partnering organisations throughout the world.

The RSC is at heart an ensemble Company. Actors, directors, dramatists
and theatre practitioners all collaborate in the creation of the RSC's
distinctive approach to theatre.

The Royal Shakespeare Company

A PARTNERSHIP WITH THE RSC

The RSC relies on the active involvement and the direct charitable support of our audience members for contributions towards our work. Members of our audience also assist by introducing us to companies, foundations and other organisations with which they have an involvement – and help us demonstrate that in return for either philanthropic or sponsorship support, we can deliver benefit to audiences, local communities, school groups and all those who are given enhanced access to our work through private sector support.

RSC PATRONS AND SHAKESPEARE'S CIRCLE

Personal contributions from RSC Patrons provide essential financial support for our artists, educationalists and their students, young writers and audience members that require special access services.

CORPORATE PARTNERSHIPS

The RSC has a global reputation, undertaking more international touring each year than any other UK arts organisation. Our profile is high; our core values of artistic excellence and outstanding performance can be aligned with commercial values and objectives.

Our extensive range of productions, outreach and education programmes help ensure that we identify the best opportunity to deliver your particular business objectives. A prestigious programme of corporate hospitality and membership packages is also available.

For more information, please telephone **01789 272283**

For detailed information about opportunities to support the work of the RSC, visit **www.rsc.org.uk/support**

This production of SIR THOMAS MORE was first performed by the Royal Shakespeare Company in the Swan Theatre, Stratford-upon-Avon, on 9 March 2005.

The original cast was as follows:

DOLL WILLIAMSON	**Michelle Butterly**
De BARD	**Kevin Harvey**
CAVELER	**Mark Springer**
WILLIAMSON	**Barry Aird**
SHERWIN	**David Hinton**
LINCOLN	**Ian Drysdale**
GEORGE BETTS	**Nigel Betts**
Clown BETTS	**Fred Ridgeway**
LORD MAYOR	**Ewen Cummins**
Sir THOMAS MORE	**Nigel Cooke**
SURESBY	**Keith Osborn**
LIFTER	**Peter Bramhill**
SMART	**Julian Stolzenberg**
Recorder	**Jon Foster**
The Earl of SHREWSBURY	**Tim Treloar**
The Earl of SURREY	**Michael Jenn**
Sir THOMAS PALMER	**James Hayes**
Sir ROBERT CHOLMLEY	**Geoffrey Freshwater**
HARRY	**Jon Foster**
ROBIN	**Julian Stolzenberg**
KIT	**Peter Bramhill**
Sir JOHN MUNDAY	**Keith Osborn**
Sheriff	**Jon Foster**
CROFTS	**Kevin Harvey**
RANDALL	**Nigel Betts**
FAULKNER	**David Hinton**
ERASMUS	**Geoffrey Freshwater**
ROPER	**Julian Stolzenberg**
Lady MORE	**Teresa Banham**
Lady ROPER	**Vinette Robinson**
MORE'S 2nd Daughter	**Miranda Colchester**
Lady MAYORESS	**Evelyn Duah**
Player	**Fred Ridgeway**
INCLINATION	**Geoffrey Freshwater**
WIT	**Nigel Betts**
Lady VANITY	**Peter Bramhill**
LUGGINS	**Ian Drysdale**
Bishop of ROCHESTER	**Keith Osborn**
Clerk of the Council	**Jon Foster**
CATESBY	**Jon Foster**
DOWNES	**Peter Bramhill**
GOUGH	**Kevin Harvey**

Poor Woman	**Michelle Butterly**
Gentleman Porter	**James Hayes**
Lieutenant of the Tower	**Mark Springer**
NED, Butler	**Ian Drysdale**
ROBIN, Brewer	**Fred Ridgeway**
RALPH, Horsekeeper	**Peter Bramhill**
GILES, Porter	**Ewen Cummins**
Messengers	**David Hinton**
	Jon Foster
	Mark Springer

All other parts played by members of the Company

Directed by	**Robert Delamere**
Designed by	**Simon Higlett**
Lighting designed by	**Wayne Dowdeswell**
Music composed by	**Ilona Sekacz**
Sound designed by	**Mike Compton**
Fights directed by	**Terry King**
Assistant Director	**Richard Twyman**
Voice & dialect work by	**Jeannette Nelson**
Casting Director	**John Cannon**
Costume Supervisor	**Christopher Porter**
Production Manager	**Simon Ash**
Company Manager	**Jondon**

Stage Manager	**Paul Sawtell**
Deputy Stage Manager	**Gabrielle Sanders**
Assistant Stage Manager	**Juliette Taylor**

The text that follows was prepared for the RSC production,
and includes material from the additions and revisions attributed
to Chettle, Heywood, Dekker and Shakespeare, as well as some sections
marked for omission from Munday and Chettle's original text.

CONTENTS

THE GUNPOWDER SEASON
Gregory Doran

In 2003 the RSC mounted a season of plays by Shakespeare's contemporaries which had rarely if ever been performed since they were written. They ranged from *Edward III*, recently 'canonised' from the apocrypha of Shakespeare, to *Eastward Ho!*, a city comedy by Jonson, Chapman and Marston, to a real discovery, a travel play by Shakespeare's collaborator John Fletcher, *The Island Princess*. Philip Massinger's *The Roman Actor* was set in the reign of the Emperor Domitian, and *The Malcontent* was a sort of revenge comedy by the anarchic John Marston.

The success of the project and the hard work of the ensemble of 28 actors and creative teams was recognised when the season transferred to the Gielgud Theatre, under the auspices of Thelma Holt and Bill Kenwright. When last were Massinger, Marston, and Fletcher on Shaftesbury Avenue? It garnered an Olivier award for the Outstanding Achievement of the Year.

I spent a great deal of time reading the astonishing number of scripts from the period and inevitably had a number of favourites which I was not able to include first time around. Indeed they would fill several more seasons to come, and will, I hope, eventually be reinvestigated by the company. We still have *The Dutch Courtesan* and *Antonio and Mellida* to tackle; along with *Philaster*, *The Sea Voyage*, and *A Trick to Catch the Old One*, *The Staple of the News* and possibly even *Hengist King of Kent*! All treasures in store! However, in considering a follow-up season I have attempted to focus the choice around the impact of the Gunpowder Plot of 1605, 400 years ago this year.

When I was at university in Bristol in the early eighties, an article in *The Observer* attracted my attention. It claimed that a new Shakespeare play had been discovered by a process of computer analysis. That play was known as *The Booke of Sir Thomas More*. I directed the play with a student company, but not as an exercise in opportunistic theatrical excavation, but because, to my amazement, the entire first half of the play concerned a race riot in the City of London. As there were race riots happening just down the road from where I lived in Bristol, in St Pauls, the play seemed particularly relevant. In the play, the riot is eventually quelled by More (in a speech universally credited to Shakespeare, as it happens to be in his own handwriting in the manuscript). The 'strangers' or foreigners to whom the citizens of London take exception were essentially religious asylum seekers, and the current heated debate over asylum makes this aspect of the play once again seem peculiarly resonant.

I am grateful to the late Peter Barnes for alerting me to Middleton and Rowley's *A New Way to Please You*, or *The Old Law*. Peter Barnes, (whose play *Jubilee*, about the Garrick Shakespeare Festival, I directed in the Swan in 2000) was a great enthusiast for the repertoire of this period. He had adapted a version of this brilliant play, for radio, and his endorsement led me to include it, and since his sad death last year, we dedicate this production to him.

The savage premise of *A New Way to Please You* is that all men at the age of eighty and all women at the age of sixty should be eradicated as no longer useful to society. It represents a strain of black comedy which it could be argued developed as a result of the sense of dislocation and a loss of moral moorings in the period following the Gunpowder Plot.

In Massinger's exceptional play *Believe What You Will*, a Middle Eastern leader comes out of hiding and attempts to rally his people, but the might of the Roman superpower hounds him from state to state, threatening any that offer him safe harbour with sanctions and ultimately war. I am grateful to Professor Martin White, our season consultant, for his suggestion that we include this strangely topical play.

Ben Jonson's tragedy *Sejanus* was published in 1605, the very year of the Gunpowder Plot. Jonson uses the Roman Empire as a metaphor for his own age. He describes the virtual police state under which he was forced to operate, with its trumped-up treason trials, and severe attitude to censorship. *Sejanus* is an extraordinary political thriller, and this production marks its first major production in four centuries.

Finally Dominic Cooke, our associate with special responsibility for new writing, commissioned Frank McGuinness to consider the events leading up to 5/11, and the result is *Speaking like Magpies*, which brings our Gunpowder season to a close.

February 2005

AUTHORSHIP AND CENSORSHIP OF 'SIR THOMAS MORE'
Martin White

The English Reformation had been accompanied by a systematic
censorship. The traditional mystery cycles were gradually
suppressed, and in 1559 a proclamation 'Prohibiting Unlicensed
Interludes and Plays, Especially on Religion or Policy' was
issued. Local authorities were ordered to ban any play in which
'either matters of religion or of the governance of the estate of
the commonwealth shall be handled or treated'. Issues of
censorship became yet more acute with the emergence in London
in the late 1560s of professional, commercial, purpose-built
playhouses, places that would bring large crowds (always a cause
of concern to the authorities) together in one place. About this
time, the Revels Office was enlarged to ensure efficient control
of plays and players, and in 1573 its chief officer, the Master of
the Revels, became the state's official censor (a role, later in the
hands of the Lord Chamberlain, that was not abolished until
1968). In 1579 Edmund Tilney became Master, and in 1581 his
powers were significantly increased by order of the Queen,
giving Tilney sole authority to license or suppress plays submitted
to him and the power to punish players or playwrights who
ignored his rulings.

The play of *Sir Thomas More* survives in a manuscript comprising
twenty-two pages, in which the hands of five anonymous
playwrights have been identified. Such authorial collaborations
were common – the account records of the theatre impresario
Philip Henslowe suggest that around half the new plays he
bought each season were collaborative efforts. Two other hands
are also present – the theatre company's Book Keeper (whose
job it was to prepare the manuscript for performance) and that
of Sir Edmund Tilney, Master of the Revels and the government
censor. Concerned at the presentation of civic disorder and
(though less so) of More's part in opposing Henry VIII's religious
reforms, Tilney demanded a substantial number of revisions,

including an instruction to 'leave out the insurrection wholly' (see Introduction to the play). The manuscript has unsurprisingly been the subject of much scholarly attention. There is a measure of agreement that the original play was the work of Anthony Munday and Henry Chettle, and was completed around 1592-4. The manuscript contains a number of rewritten and additional passages, attributed to Chettle, Heywood, Dekker and Shakespeare (the only example of his writing other than the six signatures that survive). The revisions were seemingly designed to strengthen the play theatrically, rather than just as a response to the censor's objections. While it seems evident that the additional passages post-date Tilney's censorship (the revisions do address, but don't fully meet, his objections) there are differing views on whether they date from the early 1590s or some ten years later for a revival. In fact, there is no conclusive evidence that the play was ever staged in the Elizabethan or Jacobean playhouse.

INTRODUCTION
Ann Pasternak Slater

Sir Thomas More was executed by Henry VIII in 1535. His first
biography was written by William Roper, who married More's
eldest daughter Margaret. Many details in the play of *Sir Thomas
More* originate in Roper. It gives a vividly personal, intimate
portrait of More's affectionate household. We hear More's
daughter laughing at his hair-shirt, glimpsed as he sits at supper
one summer evening in a collarless shirt. We see the king,
walking with his arm around More's neck, in the garden at
Chelsea for an hour. We hear Roper congratulating his father-
in-law on Henry's friendship, and More's shrewdly ominous
reply: 'I have no cause to be proud thereof. For if my head
would win him a castle in France, it should not fail to go.' Most
moving is Roper's description of his wife Margaret running up
to her father as he was escorted back into the Tower after his
trial, 'hastily' thrusting her way through the halberds of the
armed guard, 'openly in the sight of them all' embracing and
kissing him, turning away – and pushing back through the
crowd to run up and kiss him again. A fortnight later, on the eve
of his execution, More returns to this scene. In his last letter to
Margaret, written with charcoal saved from his fire, he tells her,
'I never liked your manners better, than when you kissed me
last. For I like when daughterly love and dear charity hath no
leisure to look to worldly courtesy.' With that letter More sent
his hair-shirt to his daughter, not wanting it to be seen when he
stripped for the executioner.

Roper tells us that Henry VIII used More as an international
negotiator because of his facility in Latin. The play strenuously
attempts to make More's dialogue seem learned by a patchy
peppering of Latin tags. More's impromptu part in the play put
on for his dinner-guests derives from Roper's account of his
improvisations in the Christmas plays of his childhood. The
precise tally of More's minimal profit from his Chancellorship
comes from Roper. So does the anecdote of his reception by the

Porter at the Tower, and the brave humour of his last exchange with his executioner – 'Pluck up thy spirits, man, and be not afraid to do thine office. My neck is very short . . . ' The play effectively perpetuates More's warm democratic persona, as witnessed by Roper and recorded by his other early biographer, Thomas Stapleton, a Catholic born in the year of More's death, who grew up among More's friends and admirers.

More's great twentieth-century biographer, R.W. Chambers, points out that the portrayal of More in this play is strikingly politically incorrect. It is based on a resilient popular tradition that defied the authority of the crown's version for the sixty years between More's death and the play's composition:

Although London has become a predominantly Protestant city, More is still its hero; at the end of the sixteenth century he is still remembered as being what the City in 1521 said he was, 'a special lover and friend in the businesses and causes of this city . . . ' Where a play gives us a view of its hero which contradicts the contemporary propaganda, it must be founded on a very strongly based and obstinate tradition.

The interesting thing is that this popular tradition pays scant attention to political questions. More's protracted conflict with Henry dwindles to some vague 'articles' he and the Bishop of Rochester refuse to sign, for which they are both imprisoned in the Tower and ultimately lose their heads. More's trial is seen exclusively through the eyes of his servants, anxiously waiting in Chelsea for news of their beloved master. The focus chosen here is characteristic of the play. More is seen as the champion of the city's mercantile and working class, not the nobility. We may think of More as the great martyr of conscience, the grave opponent of a despotic monarch. His popular reputation was the reverse. The play celebrates the 'merry, madcap More' of folk tradition. In most of its dramatised anecdotes More turns the tables against complacent authority.

This populist bias is evident in the play's dramatisation of history. The first half of the play is devoted to the anti-immigrant riot of May 1517. The characters of the rebellious crowd, their names and their precise grievances, all come accurately from the chronicler, Hall, who was a London law student at the time. Food prices were being driven up by unruly alien strangers from the continent. A Lombard had nicked a pair of pigeons bought by a carpenter called Williamson. Another abducted the wife of Sherwin the goldsmith, stole his silver, and then had the cheek to demand money for the wife's upkeep. John Lincoln, the leader of the riot, first tried legitimate complaint, asking two preachers to read a table of the citizens' grievances in the annual Easter sermon to the Mayor and Aldermen. In the uprising that followed, the crowd 'ran a-plump' through the city till they were met by More. Popular tradition, rather than history, claims that he persuaded them to return home peacefully, and engineered the pardon of those that were caught. In actual fact, 278 people, 'some men, some lads, some children of 13 years,' Hall says, were taken prisoner and thirteen were summarily hung 'in most rigorous manner'. In the play, though, the May Day riot ends with the single execution of Lincoln, its leader. His bravery before he is hanged prefigures More's courageous lightness before he is beheaded, and the first half of the play mirrors its ending. Both were popular heroes who tried to behave properly in their legitimate conflict with authority. Both die for it.

Thus, in spite of its multiple authorship, the play has a strong, simple structure. Like much drama of this period, it shrinks historical time. More's elevation from member of the king's council to knight, Privy Counsellor, and finally Lord Chancellor, follow within hours of his quelling the riot. The events of twelve years are compressed into the play's first seven scenes.

The second half is similarly accelerated. More's international reputation is epitomised in the meeting with his friend and fellow-Humanist, Erasmus, and the poet Surrey. His civic generosity is seen in his entertainment of the Lord Mayor and Aldermen. And then the downfall comes. Just as he is balanced at the top of Fortune's wheel (as the contemporary cliché would have it), summons come from the king, More refuses to sign the unspecified 'articles' and his fall rapidly follows. The second half of the play also has its significant climax, the counterpart to Lincoln's execution in the first half. The play More chooses to entertain his guests takes its title from a known Tudor interlude, *The Marriage of Wit and Wisdom*. Although it is, in fact, an amalgam of different interludes, its title neatly encapsulates More's own qualities of wise jester. And when one of the actors is late, More steps in and improvises the part of Good Counsel. The dramatic moment derives directly from the popular tradition of Tudor Morality plays and its allegorical significance would have been obvious to the most illiterate groundling. In spite of his marriage of wit and wisdom, More falls – because his good counsel contradicts the king. The play ends with Surrey's brief eulogy of More. The audience would have known that he, too, was executed before Henry's reign was over.

The continuous, solo note running through the hubbub of the play is More's voice – kindly, humorous, gracious, generous. It is heard at its best in the single scene Shakespeare unquestionably added to the play – the noisy climax of the May Day riot, and the calm brought by More's persuasive eloquence. When Shakespeare's More invokes divine and regal authority it is, as Chambers points out, a Tudor commonplace. What is memorably striking is Shakespeare's humorously sympathetic presentation of the crowd – and More's equally sympathetic appeal to their own better nature. Both Shakespeare and More appeal to the imaginations of their audience:

> Imagine that you see the wretched strangers,
> Their babies at their backs, with their poor luggage,
> Plodding to th' ports and coasts for transportation,
> And that you sit as kings in your desires . . .

Both invoke the simple Christian principle, do as you would be done by. If the king were to banish the rioters for their uprising, where would they go?

> What country, by the nature of your error,
> Should give you harbour? . . .
> Why, you must needs be strangers. Would you be pleased
> To find a nation of such barbarous temper
> That breaking out in hideous violence
> Would not afford you an abode on earth . . . ?

The text is timeless. Think of modern immigrants and asylum-seekers.

The manuscript text of *Sir Thomas More* is our only surviving play with at least one scene in Shakespeare's own handwriting. We watch him crossing out and leaving loose ends as he thinks. More than that, Tilney, Elizabeth I's Master of the Revels took an unprecedented interest in the play because of its inflammatory subject matter. In Tilney's markings we can see state censorship in practice.

The surprising thing is that Tilney was not so worried – as we might expect – by the positive presentation of More. The real danger lay in the play's sympathetic presentation of xenophobia. Popular resentment against continental immigrants remained a threat to peace in the London of the 1590s, when this play was written. Perhaps Shakespeare was called in to pre-empt Tilney's anxieties with a scene written to dissuade the contemporary London crowd from violence. But his help was sought in vain. Tilney's final, exasperated directive on the play's manuscript is explicit: 'Leave out the insurrection wholly, and the cause thereof, and begin with Sir Thomas More at the Mayor's sessions, with a report afterwards of his good service . . . a short report and not otherwise, at your own perils.' The manuscript was left untouched, a tangle of duplicate scenes in various versions and different hands, till its first publication in the mid-nineteenth century. Shakespeare's contribution was definitively identified in the 1920s. Even then the play was hardly staged. This is its first major production.

Ann Pasternak Slater is a Fellow of St Anne's College, Oxford, and author of Shakespeare the Director *(1982).*

Sir Thomas More

CHARACTERS

Sir Thomas More
Lady More, *his wife*
Master Roper, *his son-in-law*
Mistress Roper, *his elder daughter*
More's Second Daughter

Of More's House
Gough, *secretary*
Catesby, *steward*
Robin, *brewer*
Ned, *butler*
Giles, *porter*
Ralph, *horsekeeper*
Servingmen

The Earl of Shrewsbury
The Earl of Surrey
Sir Thomas Palmer
Sir Roger Cholmley
John Fisher, Bishop of Rochester

The Lord Mayor of London
The Lady Mayoress
Sir John Munday
Randall, More's Servant
Morris, *Secretary to the Bishop of Winchester*
Jack Faulkner, *his servant*
Erasmus, *friend of More*
Suresby, *a justice*
Lifter, *a cutpurse*
Smart, *plaintiff against him*
A Sheriff
Recorder

Sergeant at Arms
Clerk of the Council
Sheriffs
Officers
Justices
Ladies

John Lincoln, *a broker*
George Betts
Clown Betts, *his brother*
Williamson, *a carpenter*
Doll Williamson, *his wife*
Sherwin, *a goldsmith*
Francis de Bard, *a Lombard*
Caveler, *a Lombard*
Harry, *a prentice*
Robin, *a prentice*
Kit, *a prentice*

Crofts, a king's messenger
Downes, *an officer*
Lieutenant of the Tower
Warders of the Tower
Gentleman Porter of the Tower
Hangman
A Poor Woman

Lord Cardinal's Players
A Player (Prologue)
Inclination, *the Vice*
Lady Vanity
Lord Cardinal's Players
Luggins
Wit

ACT ONE

SCENE ONE

Enter at one end John Lincoln, with George Betts and his brother,
the Clown, at the other end enters Francis de Bard and
Doll Williamson, a lusty woman, he haling her by the arm.

Doll   Whither wilt thou hale me?

De Bard   Whither I please; thou art my prize and I plead
                purchase of thee.

Doll   Purchase of me? Away, ye rascal! I am an honest
                plain carpenter's wife, and though I have no beauty
                to like a husband, yet whatsoever is mine scorns to
                stoop to a stranger. Hand off, then, when I bid thee!

De Bard   Go with me quietly, or I'll compel thee.

Doll   Compel me, ye dog's face! Thou thinkst thou hast
                the goldsmith's wife in hand, whom thou enticedst
                from her husband with all his plate, and when thou
                turndst her home to him again, mad'st him, like an
                ass, pay for his wife's board.

De Bard   So will I make thy husband too, if please me.

Enter Caveler with a pair of doves, Williamson the carpenter,
and Sherwin following him.

Doll   Here he comes himself; tell him so if thou darest.

Caveler   Follow me no further; I say thou shalt not have
                them.

Williamson   I bought them in Cheapside, and paid my money for
                them.

Sherwin   He did, sir, indeed, and you offer him wrong, both
                to take them from him, and not restore him his
                money neither.

Caveler	If he paid for them, let it suffice that I possess them. Beef and brewis may serve such hinds. Are pigeons meat for a coarse carpenter?
Lincoln	It is hard when Englishmen's patience must be thus jetted on by strangers, and they not dare to revenge their own wrongs.
George	Lincoln, let's beat them down, and bear no more of these abuses.
Lincoln	We may not, Betts. Be patient, and hear more.
Doll	How now, husband? What, one stranger take thy food from thee, and another thy wife? By'r Lady, flesh and blood, I think, can hardly brook that.
Lincoln	Will this gear never be otherwise? Must these wrongs be thus endured?
George	Let us step in, and help to revenge their injury.
De Bard	What art thou that talkst of revenge? My lord ambassador shall once more make your mayor have a check if he punish thee for this saucy presumption.
Williamson	Indeed, my lord mayor, on the ambassador's complaint, sent me to Newgate one day because (against my will) I took the wall of a stranger. You may do anything; the goldsmith's wife, and mine now, must be at your commandment.
George	The more patient fools are ye both to suffer it.
De Bard	Suffer it? Mend it thou or he if ye can or dare. I tell thee, fellows, and she were the mayor of London's wife, had I her once in my possession, I would keep her in spite of him that durst say nay.
George	I tell thee, Lombard, these words should cost thy best cape, were I not curbed by duty and obedience. The mayor of London's wife? O God, shall it be thus?
Doll	Why, Betts, am not I as dear to my husband as my lord mayor's wife to him? – (*To Williamson*) And wilt

thou so neglectly suffer thine own shame? – (*To De Bard*) Hands off, proud stranger, or by Him that bought me, if men's milky hearts dare not strike a stranger, yet women will beat them down, ere they bear these abuses.

De Bard   Mistress, I say you shall along with me.

Doll   Touch not Doll Williamson, lest she lay thee along on God's dear earth. – (*To Caveler*) And you, sir, that allow such coarse cates to carpenters, whilst pigeons which they pay for must serve your dainty appetite: deliver them back to my husband again, or I'll call so many women to mine assistance as will not leave one inch untorn of thee. If our husbands must be bridled by law, and forced to bear your wrongs, their wives will be a little lawless, and soundly beat ye.

Caveler   Come away, De Bard, and let us go complain to my lord ambassador.

                         Exeunt Caveler and De Bard.

Doll   Ay, go, and send him among us, and we'll give him his welcome too. I am ashamed that freeborn Englishmen, having beaten strangers within their own bounds, should thus be braved and abused by them at home.

Sherwin   It is not our lack of courage in the cause, but the strict obedience that we are bound to. I am the goldsmith whose wrongs you talked of; but how to redress yours or mine own is a matter beyond our abilities.

Lincoln   Not so, not so, my good friends. I, though a mean man, a broker by profession, and named John Lincoln, have long time winked at these vile enormities with mighty impatience, and, as these two brethren here (Betts by name) can witness, with loss of mine own life would gladly remedy them.

George   And he is in a good forwardness, I tell ye, if all hit right.

Doll	As how, I prithee? Tell it to Doll Williamson.
Lincoln	You know the Spital sermons begin the next week. I have drawn a bill of our wrongs and the strangers' insolences.
George	Which he means the preachers shall there openly publish in the pulpit.
Williamson	O, but that they would! I'faith, it would tickle our strangers thoroughly.
Doll	Ay, and if you men durst not undertake it, before God, we women will. Take an honest woman from her husband? Why, it is intolerable.
Sherwin	But how find ye the preachers affected to our proceeding?
Lincoln	Master Doctor Standish hath answered that it becomes not him to move any such thing in his sermon, and tells us we must move the mayor and aldermen to reform it, and doubts not but happy success will ensue on statement of our wrongs. You shall perceive there's no hurt in the bill: here's a copy of it, I pray ye hear it.
All	With all our hearts, for God's sake read it.
Lincoln	(*Reads*) To you all, the worshipful lords and masters of this city, that will take compassion over the poor people your neighbours, and also of the great importable hurts, losses and hindrances, whereof proceedeth extreme poverty to all the king's subjects that inhabit within this city and suburbs of the same. For so it is that aliens and strangers eat the bread from the fatherless children, and take the living from all the artificers, and the intercourse from all merchants, whereby poverty is so much increased, that every man bewaileth the misery of other; for craftsmen be brought to beggary, and merchants to neediness. Wherefore, the premises considered, the redress must be of the commons, knit and united to one part. And as the hurt and damage grieveth all men,

so must all men set to their willing power for remedy,
and not suffer the said aliens in their wealth, and the
natural born men of this region to come to confusion.

Doll Before God, 'tis excellent, and I'll maintain the suit
to be honest.

Sherwin Well, say 'tis read, what is your further meaning in
the matter?

George What? Marry, list to me. No doubt but this will store
us with friends enow, whose names we will closely
keep in writing; and on May Day next in the morning
we'll go forth a-Maying, but make it the worst May
day for the strangers that ever they saw. How say ye?
Do ye subscribe, or are ye faint-hearted revolters?

Doll Hold thee, George Betts, there's my hand and my
heart; by the Lord, I'll make a captain among ye, and
do somewhat to be talk of for ever after.

Williamson My masters, ere we part, let's friendly go and drink
together, and swear true secrecy upon our lives.

George There spake an angel. Come, let us along, then.

Exeunt.

SCENE TWO

*An arras is drawn, and behind it as in sessions sit the
Lord Mayor, Justice Suresby and other Justices, Sheriff More
and the other Sheriff sitting by. Smart is the plaintiff,
Lifter the prisoner at the bar.*

Lord Mayor Having dispatched our weightier businesses,
We may give ear to petty felonies.
Master Sheriff More, what is this fellow?

More My lord, he stands indicted for a purse;
He hath been tried, the jury is together.

Lord Mayor Who sent him in?

Suresby	That did I, my lord.
	Had he had right, he had been hanged ere this;
	The only captain of the cutpurse crew.

Lord Mayor What is his name?

Suresby	As his profession is, Lifter, my lord,
	One that can lift a purse right cunningly.

Lord Mayor And is that he accuses him?

Suresby	The same, my lord, whom, by your honour's leave,
	I must say somewhat to, because I find
	In some respects he is well worthy blame.

Lord Mayor	Good master Justice Suresby, speak your mind;
	We are well pleased to give you audience.

Suresby	Hear me, Smart; thou art a foolish fellow;
	If Lifter be convicted by the law,
	As I see not how the jury can acquit him,
	I'll stand to't thou art guilty of his death.

More   My lord, that's worthy the hearing.

Lord Mayor Listen, then, good Master More.

Suresby	I tell thee plain, it is a shame for thee
	With such a sum to tempt necessity;
	No less than ten pounds, sir, will serve your turn
	To carry in your purse about with ye,
	To crake and brag in taverns of your money.
	I promise ye, a man that goes abroad
	With an intent of truth, meeting such a booty,
	May be provoked to that he never meant.
	What makes so many pilferers and felons,
	But such fond baits that foolish people lay
	To tempt the needy miserable wretch?
	Ten pounds odd money; this is a pretty sum
	To bear about, which were more safe at home.
	Fore God, 'twere well to fine ye as much more

Lord Mayor and More whisper.

To the relief of the poor prisoners,
To teach ye be more careful of your own.

	In sooth, I say ye were but rightly served, If ye had lost as much as twice ten pounds.
More	Good my lord, soothe a point or two for once, Only to try conclusions in this case.
Lord Mayor	Content, good Master More. – We'll rise awhile, And till the jury can return their verdict Walk in the garden. How say ye, justices?
All	We like it well, my lord; we'll follow ye.

Exeunt Lord Mayor and Justices.

More	Nay, plaintiff, go you too: *Exit Smart.*
	and officers, Stand you aside, and leave the prisoner To me awhile. – Lifter, come hither.
Lifter	What is your worship's pleasure?
More	Sirrah, you know that you are known to me, And I have often saved ye from this place Since first I came in office: thou seest beside, That Justice Suresby is thy heavy friend, By all the blame that he pretends to Smart For tempting thee with such a sum of money. I tell thee what; devise me but a means To pick or cut his purse, and, on my credit, And as I am a Christian and a man, I will procure thy pardon for that jest.
Lifter	Good master shrieve, seek not my overthrow. You know, sir, I have many heavy friends, And more indictments like to come upon me. You are too deep for me to deal withal; You are known to be one of the wisest men That is in England. I pray ye, master sheriff, Go not about to undermine my life.
More	Lifter, I am true subject to my king. Thou much mistak'st me, and, for thou shalt not think I mean by this to hurt thy life at all,

I will maintain the act when thou hast done it.
Thou knowest there are such matters in my hands
As, if I pleased to give them to the jury,
I should not need this way to circumvent thee.
All that I aim at is a merry jest:
Perform it, Lifter, and expect my best.

Lifter   I thank your worship, God preserve your life.
But master Justice Suresby is gone in;
I know not how to come near where he is.

More   Let me alone for that, I'll be thy setter;
I'll send him hither to thee presently
Under the colour of thine own request
Of private matters to acquaint him with.

Lifter   If ye do so, sir, then let me alone:
Forty to one but then his purse is gone.

More   Well said, but see that thou diminish not
One penny of the money, but give it me.
It is the cunning act that credits thee.

Lifter   I will, good master Sheriff, I assure ye.

Exit More.

I see the purpose of this gentleman
Is but to check the folly of the justice
For blaming others in a desperate case,
Wherein himself may fall as soon as any.
To save my life it is a good adventure.
Silence there ho! Now doth the justice enter.

Enter Justice Suresby.

Suresby   Now, sirrah, now, what is your will with me?
Wilt thou discharge thy conscience like an honest
man?
What sayst to me, sirrah? Be brief, be brief.

Lifter   As brief, sir, as I can. –
(*Aside*) If ye stand fair, I will be brief anon.

Suresby   Speak out, and mumble not; what sayst thou, sirrah?

Lifter	Sir, I am charged, as God shall be my comfort,
	With more than's true.
Suresby	Sir, sir, ye are indeed, 'with more than's true',
	For you are flatly charged with felony.
	You're charged with more than truth, and that is theft;
	More than a true man should be charged withal.
	Thou art a varlet, that's no more than true.
	Trifle not with me; do not, do not, sirrah;
	Confess but what thou knowest, I ask no more.
Lifter	There be, sir, there be, if't shall please your worship –
Suresby	There be, varlet? What be there? Tell me what there be.
	Come off or on, there be, what be there, knave?
Lifter	There be, sir, diverse very cunning fellows
	That while you stand and look them in the face
	Will have your purse.
Suresby	Th'art an honest knave.
	Tell me what are they? Where they may be caught?
	Ay, those are they I look for.
Lifter	You talk of me, sir.
	Alas, I am a puny! There's one indeed
	Goes by my name, he puts down all for purses;
	He'll steal your worship's purse under your nose.
Suresby	Be as familiar as thou wilt, my knave;
	'Tis this I long to know.
Lifter	(*Aside*) And you shall have your longing ere ye go. –
	This fellow, sir, perhaps will meet ye thus,
	Or thus, or thus, and in kind compliment
	Pretend acquaintance, somewhat doubtfully;
	And these embraces serve –
Suresby	(*Shrugging gladly*) Ay, marry, Lifter,
	Wherefor serve they?
Lifter	Only to feel
	Whether you go full under sail or no,
	Or that your lading be aboard your bark.

Suresby	In plainer English, Lifter, if my purse Be stored or no?
Lifter	Ye have it, sir.
Suresby	Excellent, excellent.
Lifter	Then, sir, you cannot but for manners' sake Walk on with him, for he will walk your way, Alleging either you have much forgot him, Or he mistakes you.
Suresby	But in this time has he my purse or no?
Lifter	Not yet, sir, fie!

Enter Lord Mayor, Justices and More.

No, nor I have not yours. –
But now we must forbear; my lords return.

Suresby	A murrain on't! Lifter, we'll more anon. Ay, thou sayst true, there are shrewd knaves indeed.

He sits down.

But let them gull me, widgeon me, rook me, fop me!
I'faith, i'faith, they are too short for me.
Knaves and fools meet when purses go,
Wise men look to their purses well enow.

More	(*To Lifter*) Lifter, is it done?
Lifter	(*To More*) Done, master shrieve; and there it is.
More	(*To Lifter*) Then build upon my word. I'll save thy life.
Recorder	Lifter, stand to the bar. The jury have returned thee guilty. Thou must die, According to the custom. – Look to it, master shrieve.
Lord Mayor	Then, gentlemen, as you are wont to do, Because as yet we have no burial place, What charity your meaning's to bestow Toward burial of the prisoners now condemned, Let it be given. There is first for me.
Recorder	And there's for me.

More	And me.
Suresby	Body of me, my purse is gone!
More	Gone, sir? What, here? How can that be?
Lord Mayor	Against all reason, sitting on the bench.
Suresby	Lifter, I talked with you; you have not lifted me, ha?
Lifter	Suspect ye me, sir? O what a world is this!
More	But hear ye, master Suresby; are ye sure Ye had a purse about ye?
Suresby	Sure, master shrieve, as sure as you are there, And in it seven pounds odd money, on my faith.
More	Seven pounds, odd money! What, were you so mad, Being a wise man and a magistrate, To trust your purse with such a liberal sum? Seven pounds odd money! 'Fore God, it is a shame With such a sum to tempt necessity. I promise ye, a man that goes abroad With an intent of truth, meeting such a booty, May be provoked to that he never thought. What makes so many pilferers and felons, But these fond baits that foolish people lay To tempt the needy miserable wretch? Should he be taken now that has your purse, I'd stand to't, you are guilty of his death, For questionless he would be cast by law. 'Twere a good deed to fine ye as much more To the relief of the poor prisoners, To teach ye lock your money up at home.
Suresby	Well, Master More, you are a merry man; I find ye, sir, I find ye well enough.
More	Nay, ye shall see, sir, trusting thus your money, And Lifter here in trial for like case, But that the poor man is a prisoner It would be now suspected that he had it. Thus may ye see what mischief often comes By the fond carriage of such needless sums.

Lord Mayor   Believe me, Master Suresby, this is strange,
  You, being a man so settled in assurance,
  Will fall in that which you condemned in other.

More   Well, Master Suresby, there's your purse again,
  And all your money. Fear nothing of More:
  Wisdom still keeps the mean and locks the door.

Exeunt.

SCENE THREE

*Enter the Earls of Shrewsbury and Surrey, Sir Thomas Palmer
and Sir Roger Cholmley.*

Shrewsbury   My Lord of Surrey, and Sir Thomas Palmer,
  Might I with patience tempt your grave advice?
  I tell ye true, that in these dangerous times
  I do not like this frowning vulgar brow.
  My searching eye did never entertain
  A more distracted countenance of grief
  Than I have late observed
  In the displeasèd commons of the city.

Surrey   'Tis strange that from his princely clemency,
  So well a tempered mercy and a grace
  To all the aliens in this fruitful land,
  That this high-crested insolence should spring
  From them that breathe from his majestic bounty,
  That, fattened with the traffic of our country,
  Already leaps into his subjects' face.

Palmer   Yet Sherwin, hindered to commence his suit
  Against De Bard by the ambassador,
  By supplication made unto the king,
  Who having first enticed away his wife
  And got his plate, near worth four hundred pound,
  To grieve some wronged citizens that found
  This vile disgrace oft cast into their teeth,
  Of late sues Sherwin, and arrested him
  For money for the boarding of his wife.

Surrey	The more knave Bard, that, using Sherwin's goods Doth ask him interest for the occupation. I like not that, my lord of Shrewsbury. He's ill bested that lends a well-paced horse Unto a man that will not find him meat.
Cholmley	My lord of Surrey will be pleasant still.
Palmer	I being then employed by your honours To stay the broil that fell about the same, Where by persuasion I enforced the wrongs And urged the grief of the displeasèd city, He answered me, and with a solemn oath, That, if he had the Mayor of London's wife, He would keep her in despite of any English.
Surrey	'Tis good, Sir Thomas, then, for you and me; Your wife is dead and I a bachelor. If no man can possess his wife alone, I am glad, Sir Thomas Palmer, I have none.
Cholmley	If 'a take my wife, 'a shall find her meat.
Surrey	And reason good, Sir Roger Cholmley, too. If these hot Frenchmen needsly will have sport, They should in kindness yet defray the charge. 'Tis hard when men possess our wives in quiet And yet leave us in to discharge their diet.
Shrewsbury	My lord, our caters shall not use the market For our provision, but some stranger now Will take the victuals from him he hath bought. A carpenter, as I was late informed, Who having bought a pair of doves in Cheap, Immediately a Frenchman took them from him And beat the poor man for resisting him, And when the fellow did complain his wrongs, He was severely punished for his labour.
Surrey	But if the English blood be once but up, As I perceive their hearts already full, I fear me much, before their spleens be cold, Some of these saucy aliens for their pride Will pay for 't soundly, wheresoe'er it lights.

This tide of rage that with the eddy strives,
I fear me much, will drown too many lives.

Cholmley   Now, afore God, your honours, pardon me:
Men of your place and greatness are to blame.
I tell ye true, my lords, in that his majesty
Is not informèd of this base abuse
And daily wrongs are offered to his subjects.
For if he were, I know his gracious wisdom
Would soon redress it.

Enter a Messenger.

Shrewsbury   Sirrah, what news?

Cholmley   None good, I fear.

Messenger   My lord, ill news, and worse, I fear, will follow
If speedily it be not looked unto.
The city is in an uproar, and the mayor
Is threatened if he come out of his house.
A number poor artificers are up
In arms and threaten to avenge their wrongs.

Cholmley   We feared what this would come unto:
This follows on the doctor's publishing
The bill of wrongs in public at the Spital.

Shrewsbury   That Doctor Beale may chance beshrew himself
For reading of the bill.

Palmer   Let us go gather forces to the mayor
For quick suppressing this rebellious rout.

Surrey   Now I bethink myself of Master More,
One of the sheriffs, a wise and learned gentleman,
And in especial favour with the people.
He, backed with other grave and sober men,
May by his gentle and persuasive speech
Perhaps prevail more than we can with power.

Shrewsbury   Believe me but your honour well advises.
Let us make haste, for I do greatly fear
Some to their graves this morning's work will bear.

Exeunt.

ACT TWO

SCENE ONE

Enter three or four Apprentices of trades, with a pair of cudgels.

Harry	Come, lay down the cudgels. – Ho, Robin, you met us well at Bunhill, to have you with us a-Maying this morning.
Robin	Faith, Harry, the head drawer at the Mitre by the Great Conduit called me up, and we went to breakfast into St. Anne's Lane. But come, who begins? In good faith, I am clean out of practice. When wast at Garrett's school, Harry?
Harry	Not this great while, never since I brake his usher's head, when he played his scholar's prize at the Star in Bread Street. I use all to George Philpot's at Dowgate; he's the best backsword man in England.
Kit	Bate me an ace of that, quoth Bolton.
Harry	I'll not bate ye a pin on't, sir; for by this cudgel 'tis true.
Kit	I will cudgel that opinion out of ye: did you break an usher's head, sir?
Harry	Ay, marry, did I, sir.
Kit	I am very glad on't; you shall break mine too, and ye can.
Harry	Sirrah, I prithee, what art thou?
Kit	Why, I am a prentice as thou art; seest thou now? I'll play with thee at blunt here in Cheapside, and when thou hast done, if thou beest angry, I'll fight with thee at sharp in Moorfields. I have a sword to serve my turn in a favour.

Exeunt.

SCENE TWO

Enter Lincoln, George Betts, the Clown, Williamson,
Sherwin and other armed; Doll in a shirt of mail, a headpiece,
sword and buckler; a crew attending.

Clown	Come, come, we'll tickle their turnips, we'll butter their boxes. Shall strangers rule the roost? Yes, but we'll baste the roost. Come, come, a flaunt, a flaunt!
George	Brother, give place and hear John Lincoln speak.
Clown	Ay, Lincoln my leader,

And Doll my true breeder,
With the rest of our crew,
Shall rantantarraran,
Do all they what they can.
Shall we be bobbed, braved? No.
Shall we be held under? No.
We are free born
And do take scorn
To be used so.

Doll	Peace there, I say! Hear captain Lincoln speak; keep silence, till we know his mind at large.
Clown	Then largely deliver: speak, bully: and he that presumes to interrupt thee in thy oration, this for him!
Lincoln	Then, gallant bloods, you whose free souls do scorn

To bear th'enforcèd wrongs of aliens,
Add rage to resolution, fire the houses
Of these audacious strangers. This is St. Martin's,
And yonder dwells Meautis, a wealthy Picard,
At the Green Gate,
De Bard, Peter van Hollock, Adrian Martin,
With many more outlandish fugitives.
Shall these enjoy more privilege than we
In our own country? Let's then become their slaves.
Since justice keeps not them in greater awe,
We'll be ourselves rough ministers at law.

Clown	Use no more swords, nor no more words, but fire the houses; brave captain courageous, fire me their houses.
Doll	Ay, for we may as well make bonfires on May day as at midsummer; we'll alter the day in the calendar, and set it down in flaming letters.
Sherwin	Stay! That would much endanger the whole city, Whereto I would not the least prejudice.
Doll	No, nor I neither; so may mine own house be burned for company. I'll tell ye what: we'll drag the strangers into Moorfields, and there bombast them till they stink again.
Clown	And that's soon done, for they smell for fear already.
George	Let some of us enter the strangers' houses, And if we find them there, then bring them forth.
Doll	But if ye bring them forth ere ye find them, I'll ne'er allow of that.
Clown	Now, Mars, for thy honour, Dutch or French, So it be a wench, I'll upon her.

Exeunt some and Sherwin.

Williamson	Now, lads, how shall we labour in our safety? I hear the mayor hath gathered men in arms, And that shrieve More an hour ago received Some of the Privy Council in at Ludgate. Force now must make our peace, or else we fall: 'Twill soon be known we are the principal.
Doll	And what of that? If thou beest afraid, husband, go home again, and hide thy head for, by the Lord, I'll have a little sport now we are at it.
George	Let's stand upon our guard, and if they come, Receive them as they were our enemies.

Enter Sherwin and the rest.

Clown	A purchase, a purchase! We have found, we ha' found –
Doll	What?
Clown	Nothing; not a French Fleming nor a Fleming French to be found, but all fled in plain English.
Lincoln	How now! Have you found any?
Sherwin	No, not one; they're all fled.
Lincoln	Then fire the houses, that the mayor being busy About the quenching of them, we may 'scape. Burn down their kennels. Let us straight away, Least this day prove to us an ill May day.
Clown	Fire, fire! I'll be the first: If hanging come, tis welcome; that's the worst.

Exeunt.

SCENE THREE

Enter at one door Sir Thomas More and Lord Mayor; at another door Sir John Munday hurt.

Lord Mayor What, Sir John Munday, are you hurt?

Sir John	A little knock, my lord. There was even now A sort of prentices playing at cudgels. I did command them to their masters' houses, But now, I fear me, they are gone to join With Lincoln, Sherwin, and their dangerous train.
More	The captains of this insurrection Have taken themselves to arms and came but now To both the Counters where they have released Sundry indebted prisoners, and from thence I hear that they are gone into St. Martin's, Where they intend to offer violence To the amazed Lombards. Therefore, my lord,

If we expect the safety of the city,
'Tis time that force or parley do encounter
With these displeasèd men.

Enter a Messenger.

Lord Mayor How now, what news?

Messenger My lord, the rebels have broke open Newgate,
From whence they have delivered many prisoners,
Both felons and notorious murderers,
That desperately cleave to their lawless train.

Lord Mayor Up with the drawbridge, gather some forces
To Cornhill and Cheapside: – and, gentlemen,
If diligence be weighed on every side,
A quiet ebb will follow this rough tide.

Enter Shrewsbury, Surrey, Palmer, and Cholmley.

Shrewsbury Lord Mayor, his majesty, receiving notice
Of this most dangerous insurrection,
Hath sent my lord of Surrey and myself,
Sir Thomas Palmer and our followers,
To add unto your forces our best means
For pacifying of this mutiny.
In God's name then, set on with happy speed:
The king laments if one true subject bleed.

Surrey I hear they mean to fire the Lombards' houses.
O power, what art thou in a madman's eyes:
Thou mak'st the plodding idiot bloody wise.

More My lords, I doubt not but we shall appease
With a calm breath this flux of discontent:

Palmer To call them to a parley questionless
May fall out good. 'Tis well said, Master More.

More Let's to these simple men; for many sweat
Under this act that knows not the law's debt
Which hangs upon their lives. For silly men
Plod on they know not how, like a fool's pen
That ending shows not any sentence writ,
Linked but to common reason or slightest wit.

These follow for no harm, but yet incur
Self penalty with those that raised this stir.
A God's name on, to calm our private foes
With breath of gravity, not dangerous blows.

Exeunt.

SCENE FOUR

Enter Lincoln, Doll, Clown, George Betts, Williamson,
others and a Sergeant at Arms.

Lincoln	Peace, hear me: he that will not see a red herring at a Harry groat, butter at eleven pence a pound, meal at nine shillings a bushel, and beef at four nobles a stone, list to me.
George	It will come to that pass, if strangers be suffered. Mark him.
Lincoln	Our country is a great eating country; *argo* they eat more in our country than they do in their own.
Clown	By a halfpenny loaf a day troy weight.
Lincoln	They bring in strange roots, which is merely to the undoing of poor prentices, for what's a sorry parsnip to a good heart?
Williamson	Trash, trash! They breed sore eyes, and 'tis enough to infect the city with the palsy.
Lincoln	Nay, it has infected it with the palsy; for these bastards of dung – as you know they grow in dung – have infected us, and it is our infection will make the city shake, which partly comes through the eating of parsnips.
Clown	True, and pumpkins together.
Sergeant	What say ye to the mercy of the king? Do you refuse it?

Lincoln	You would have us upon th'hip, would you? No, marry, do we not; we accept of the king's mercy, but we will show no mercy upon the strangers.
Sergeant	You are the simplest things that ever stood In such a question.
Lincoln	How say ye now, prentices? Prentices simple? Down with him!
All	Prentices simple, prentices simple!

Enter the Lord Mayor, Surrey, Shrewsbury, More.

Lord Mayor	Hold, in the king's name, hold!
Surrey	Friends, masters, countrymen –
Lord Mayor	Peace, ho, peace! I charge you, keep the peace!
Shrewsbury	My masters, countrymen –
Williamson	The noble Earl of Shrewsbury, let's hear him.
George	We'll hear the Earl of Surrey.
Lincoln	The Earl of Shrewsbury.
George	We'll hear both.
All	Both, both, both, both!
Lincoln	Peace, I say, peace! Are you men of wisdom, or what are you?
Surrey	What you will have them, but not men of wisdom.
Some Citizens	We'll not hear my lord of Surrey!
Others	No, no, no, no, no, Shrewsbury, Shrewsbury!
More	Whiles they are o'er the bank of their obedience Thus will they bear down all things.
Lincoln	Shrieve More speaks. Shall we hear Shrieve More speak?
Doll	Let's hear him. 'A keeps a plentiful shrievalty, and 'a made my brother, Arthur Watchins, Sergeant Safe's yeoman. Let's hear Shrieve More.

All	Shrieve More, More, More, Shrieve More!
More	Even by the rule you have among yourselves, Command still audience.
Some	Surrey, Surrey!
Others	More, More!
Lincoln	Peace, peace, silence, peace.
George	Peace, peace, silence, peace.
More	You that have voice and credit with the number, Command them to a stillness.
Lincoln	A plague on them, they will not hold their peace; the devil cannot rule them.
More	Then what a rough and riotous charge have you, To lead those that the devil cannot rule. – Good masters, hear me speak.
Doll	Ay by th'mass will we, More. Th'art a good housekeeper, and I thank thy good worship for my brother Arthur Watchins.
All	Peace, peace!
More	Look what you do offend you cry upon, That is, the peace; not one of you here present, Had there such fellows lived when you were babes, That could have topped the peace, as now you would. The peace wherein you have till now grown up Had been ta'en from you, and the bloody times Could not have brought you to the state of men. Alas, poor things, what is it you have got, Although we grant you get the thing you seek?
George	Marry, the removing of the strangers, which cannot choose but much advantage the poor handicrafts of the city.
More	Grant them removed, and grant that this your noise Hath chid down all the majesty of England. Imagine that you see the wretched strangers, Their babies at their backs, with their poor luggage,

Plodding to th' ports and coasts for transportation,
And that you sit as kings in your desires,
Authority quite silenced by your brawl,
And you in ruff of your opinions clothed:
What had you got? I'll tell you: you had taught
How insolence and strong hand should prevail,
How order should be quelled, and by this pattern
Not one of you should live an aged man,
For other ruffians, as their fancies wrought,
With self same hand, self reasons and self right,
Would shark on you, and men like ravenous fishes
Would feed on one another.

Doll	Before God, that's as true as the Gospel.
George	Nay, this is a sound fellow, I tell you: let's mark him.
More	Let me set up before your thoughts, good friends,

One supposition, which if you will mark
You shall perceive how horrible a shape
Your innovation bears. First, 'tis a sin
Which oft th'apostle did forewarn us of,
Urging obedience to authority,
And 'twere no error, if I told you all,
You were in arms against God Himself.

All	Marry, God forbid that.
More	Nay, certainly you are,

For to the king God hath His office lent
Of dread, of justice, power and command,
Hath bid him rule, and willed you to obey;
And to add ampler majesty to this,
He hath not only lent the king His figure,
His throne and sword, but given him His own name,
Calls him a god on earth. What do you, then,
Rising 'gainst him that God Himself installs,
But rise 'gainst God? What do you to your souls
In doing this, O desperate as you are?
Wash your foul minds with tears, and those same
                                                    hands
That you like rebels lift against the peace
Lift up for peace, and your unreverent knees

Make them your feet. To kneel to be forgiven
Is safer wars than ever you can make
Whose discipline is riot.
What rebel captain,
As mutinies are incident, by his name
Can still the rout? Who will obey a traitor?
Or how can well that proclamation sound
When there is no addition but a rebel
To qualify a rebel? You'll put down strangers,
Kill them, cut their throats, possess their houses,
And lead the majesty of law in lyam,
To slip him like a hound. Say now the king
(As he is clement if th'offender mourn)
Should so much come too short of your great trespass
As but to banish you, whither would you go?
What country, by the nature of your error,
Should give you harbour? Go you to France or
                                 Flanders,
To any German province, to Spain or Portugal,
Nay, anywhere that not adheres to England,
Why, you must needs be strangers. Would you be
                                 pleased
To find a nation of such barbarous temper
That breaking out in hideous violence
Would not afford you an abode on earth,
Whet their detested knives against your throats,
Spurn you like dogs, and like as if that God
Owed not nor made not you, nor that the elements
Were not all appropriate to your comforts,
But chartered unto them? What would you think
To be thus used? This is the strangers' case,
And this your mountanish inhumanity.

All	Faith, 'a says true; let's do as we may be done by.
Lincoln	We'll be ruled by you, Master More, if you'll stand our friend to procure our pardon.
More	Submit you to these noble gentlemen, Entreat their mediation to the king, Give up yourself to form, obey the magistrate, And there's no doubt but mercy may be found,

If you so seek it.
To persist in it is present death: but, if you
Yield yourselves, no doubt what punishment
You in simplicity have incurred, his highness
In mercy will most graciously pardon.

All   We yield, and desire his highness' mercy.

They lay by their weapons.

More   No doubt his majesty will grant it you.
But you must yield to go to several prisons,
Till that his highness' will be further known.

All   Most willingly; whither you will have us.

Shrewsbury Lord Mayor, let them be sent to several prisons,
And there, in any case, be well entreated.
My lord of Surrey, please you to take horse
And ride to Cheapside, where the aldermen
Are with their several companies in arms.
Will them to go unto their several wards,
Both for the stay of further mutiny,
And for the apprehending of such persons
As shall contend.

Surrey   I go, my noble lord.   *Exit.*

Shrewsbury We'll straight go tell his highness these good news;
Withal, Shrieve More, I'll tell him how your breath
Hath ransomed many a subject from sad death.

Exit Shrewsbury and Cholmley.

Lord Mayor Lincoln and Sherwin, you shall both to Newgate,
The rest unto the Counters.

Palmer   Go guard them hence: a little breath well spent
Cheats expectation in his fairest event.

Doll   Well, Sheriff More, thou hast done more with thy
good words than all they could with their weapons.
Give me thy hand; keep thy promise now for the
king's pardon, or, by the Lord, I'll call thee a plain
cony-catcher.

Lincoln	Farewell, Shrieve More; and as we yield by thee,
	So make our peace, then thou dealst honestly.
Clown	Ay, and save us from the gallows, else 'a deals double
	honestly!

They are led away.

Lord Mayor Master Shrieve More, you have preserved the city
From a most dangerous fierce commotion,
For if this limb of riot here in St. Martin's
Had joined with other branches of the city
That did begin to kindle, 'twould have bred
Great rage, that rage much murder would have fed.
Not steel, but eloquence hath wrought this good:
You have redeemed us from much threatened blood.

More   My lord and brethren, what I here have spoke,
My country's love, and next the city's care
Enjoined me to, which since it thus prevails,
Think, God hath made weak More his instrument
To thwart sedition's violent intent.
I think 'twere best, my lord, some two hours hence
We meet at the Guildhall, and there determine
That thorough every ward the watch be clad
In armour, but especially provide
That at the city gates selected men,
Substantial citizens, do ward tonight
For fear of further mischief.

Lord Mayor   It shall be so:
But yond methink's my lord of Shrewsbury.

Enter Shrewsbury.

Shrewsbury My lord, his majesty sends loving thanks
To you, your brethren, and his faithful subjects,
Your careful citizens. But Master More, to you
A rougher, yet as kind, a salutation:
Your name is yet too short, nay, you must kneel,
A knight's creation is this knightly steel.
Rise up, Sir Thomas More.

More   I thank his highness for thus honouring me.

Shrewsbury   This is but first taste of his princely favour,
             For it hath pleased his high majesty
             (Noting your wisdom and deserving merit)
             To put this staff of honour in your hand,
             For he hath chose you of his Privy Council.

More   My lord, for to deny my sovereign's bounty
             Were to drop precious stones into the heaps
             Whence they first came;
             To urge my imperfections in excuse,
             Were all as stale as custom. No, my lord,
             My service is my king's, good reason why,
             Since life or death hangs on our sovereign's eye.

Lord Mayor   His majesty hath honoured much the city
             In this his princely choice.

More   My lord and brethren,
             Though I depart for court my love shall rest
             With you, as heretofore, a faithful guest.
             I now must sleep in court, sound sleeps forbear:
             The chamberlain to state is public care.
             Yet in this rising of my private blood,
             My studious thoughts shall tend the city's good.

                        Enter Crofts.

Shrewsbury   How now, Crofts? What news?

Crofts   My lord, his highness sends express command
             That a record be entered of this riot,
             And that the chief and capital offenders
             Be thereon straight arraigned, for himself intends
             To sit in person on the rest tomorrow
             At Westminster.

Shrewsbury   Lord Mayor, you hear your charge.
             Come, good Sir Thomas More, to court let's hie;
             You are th'appeaser of this mutiny.

More   My lord, farewell, new days begets new tides;
             Life whirls 'bout fate, then to a grave it slides.

                                              Exeunt.

SCENE FIVE

Enter Sheriff, and meets a Messenger.

Sheriff	Messenger, what news?
Messenger	Is execution yet performed?
Sheriff	Not yet; the carts stand ready at the stairs, And they shall presently away to Tyburn.
Messenger	Stay master shrieve, it is the council's pleasure, For more example in so bad a case, A gibbet be erected in Cheapside, Hard by the Standard, whither you must bring Lincoln and those that were the chief with him, To suffer death, and that immediately.

Enter Officers.

Sheriff	It shall be done, sir. *Exit Messenger.* Officers, be speedy; Call for a gibbet, see it be erected; Others make haste to Newgate, bid them bring The prisoners hither, for they here must die. Away I say, and see no time be slacked.
Officers	We go, sir.

Exeunt some severally; others set up the gibbet.

Sheriff	That's well said, fellows; now you do your duty. God for his pity help these troublous times. The street's stopped up with gazing multitudes: Command our armèd officers with halberds Make way for entrance of the prisoners. Let proclamation once again be made That every householder, on pain of death, Keep in his prentices, and every man Stand with a weapon ready at his door, As he will answer to the contrary.
Officer	I'll see it done, sir.

Exit.

Enter another Officer.

Sheriff	Bring them away to execution:
	The writ is come above two hours since;
	The city will be fined for this neglect.

Officer	There's such a press and multitude at Newgate,
	They cannot bring the carts unto the stairs,
	To take the prisoners in.

Sheriff	Then let them come on foot;
	We may not dally time with great command.

Officer	Some of the Bench, sir, think it very fit
	That stay be made, and give it out abroad
	The execution is deferred till morning,
	And, when the streets shall be a little cleared,
	To chain them up, and suddenly dispatch it.

The Prisoners are brought in well guarded.

Sheriff	Stay; in mean time methinks they come along.
	See, they are coming. So,'tis very well:
	Bring Lincoln there the first unto the tree.

Clown	Ay, for I cry lag, sir.

Lincoln	I knew the first, sir, did belong to me.
	This the old proverb now complete doth make,
	That Lincoln should be hanged for London's sake.

He goes up.

A God's name, let's to work. Fellow, dispatch:
I was the foremost man in this rebellion,
And I the foremost that must die for it.

Doll	Bravely, John Lincoln, let thy death express
	That, as thou livedst a man, thou diedst no less.

Lincoln	Doll Williamson, thine eyes shall witness it.
	Then to all you that come to view mine end
	I must confess I had no ill intent,
	But against such as wronged us over much.
	And now I can perceive it was not fit
	That private men should carve out their redress,

Which way they list; no, learn it now by me,
Obedience is the best in each degree.
And asking mercy meekly of my king,
I patiently submit me to the law.
But God forgive them that were cause of it,
And as a Christian truly from my heart
I likewise crave they would forgive me too
(As freely as I do forgive their wrong)
That others by example of the same
Henceforth be warnèd to attempt the like
'Gainst any alien that repaireth hither.
Fare ye well, all: the next time that we meet,
I trust in heaven we shall each other greet.

He leaps off.

Doll	Farewell, John Lincoln; say all what they can,
	Thou livedst a good fellow, and diedst an honest man.
Clown	Would I were so far on my journey: the first stretch
	is the worst, methinks.
Sheriff	Bring Williamson there forward.
Doll	Good Master Shrieve, I have an earnest suit,
	And as you are a man deny't me not.
Sheriff	Woman, what is it? Be it in my power,
	Thou shalt obtain it.
Doll	Let me die next sir, that is all I crave.
	You know not what a comfort you shall bring
	To my poor heart to die before my husband.
Sheriff	Bring her to death; she shall have her desire.
Clown	Sir, and I have a suit for you too.
Sheriff	What is it?
Clown	That, as you have hanged Lincoln first, and will hang
	her next, so you will not hang me at all.
Sheriff	Nay, you set ope the Counter gates, and you must
	hang for the folly.
Clown	Well, then, so much for it.

Doll   Sir, your free bounty much contents my mind.
              Commend me to that good shrieve Master More,
              And tell him had't not been for his persuasion
              John Lincoln had not hung here as he does.
              We would first have locked us up in Leaden Hall
              And there been burned to ashes with the roof.

Sheriff   Woman, what Master More did was a subject's duty,
              And hath so pleased our gracious lord the king,
              That he is hence removed to higher place
              And made of council to his majesty.

Doll   Well is he worthy of it, by my troth,
              An honest, wise, well spoken gentleman;
              Yet would I praise his honesty much more
              If he had kept his word, and saved our lives.
              But let that pass; men are but men, and so
              Words are but words, and pays not what men owe.
              Now, husband, since perhaps the world may say
              That through my means thou comest thus to thy end,
              Here I begin this cup of death to thee,
              Because thou shalt be sure to taste no worse
              Than I have taken that must go before thee.
              What though I be a woman? That's no matter;
              I do owe God a death, and I must pay him.
              Husband, give me thy hand; be not dismayed;
              This char being charred, then all our debt is paid.
              Only two little babes we leave behind us,
              And all I can bequeath them at this time
              Is but the love of some good honest friend
              To bring them up in charitable sort.
              What, masters, he goes upright that never halts,
              And they may live to mend their parents' faults.

Williamson Why, well said, wife. I'faith, thou cheerst my heart.
              Give me thy hand; let's kiss, and so let's part.

                                        He kisses her on the ladder.

Doll   The next kiss, Williamson, shall be in heaven.
              Now cheerily, lads. George Betts, a hand with thee,
              And thine too, Ralph, and thine, good honest Sherwin.
              Now let me tell the women of this town

No stranger yet brought Doll to lying down.
So long as I an Englishman can see,
Nor French nor Dutch shall get a kiss of me;
And when that I am dead, for me yet say
I died in scorn to be a stranger's prey.

A great shout and noise.

Enter Surrey.

Surrey	Save the man's life, if it be possible.
Sheriff	It is too late, my lord; he's dead already.
Surrey	I tell ye, master sheriff, you are too forward,
	To make such haste with men unto their death;
	I think your pains will merit little thanks,
	Since that his highness is so merciful
	As not to spill the blood of any subject.
Sheriff	My noble lord, would we so much had known,
	The Council's warrant hastened our dispatch;
	It had not else been done so suddenly.
Surrey	Sir Thomas More humbly upon his knee
	Did beg the lives of all, since on his word
	They did so gently yield: the king hath granted it,
	And made him Lord High Chancellor of England,
	According as he worthily deserves.
	Since Lincoln's life cannot be had again,
	Then for the rest, from my dread sovereign's lips,
	I here pronounce free pardon for them all.
All	God save the king, God save the king,
	My good Lord Chancellor, and the Earl of Surrey.

Flinging up caps.

Doll	And Doll desires it from her very heart,
	More's name may live for this right noble part;
	And whenso'er we talk of ill May day,
	Praise More.
Surrey	In hope his highness' clemency and mercy,
	Which in the arms of mild and meek compassion
	Would rather clip you, as the loving nurse

Oft doth the wayward infant, than to leave you
To the sharp rod of justice, so to draw you
To shun such lewd assemblies as beget
Unlawful riots and such traitorous acts,
That, striking with the hand of private hate,
Maim your dear country with a public wound.
O God, that Mercy, whose majestic brow
Should be unwrinkled, and that awful Justice,
Which looketh through a veil of sufferance
Upon the frailty of the multitude,
Should with the clamours of outrageous wrongs
Be stirred and wakened thus to punishment!
But your deservèd death he doth forgive:
Who gives you life, pray all he long may live.

All   God save the king, God save the king,
My good Lord Chancellor, and the Earl of Surrey.

Exeunt.

ACT THREE

SCENE ONE

A table being covered with a green carpet, a state cushion on it,
and the Purse and Mace lying thereon, enter Sir Thomas More.

More   It is in heaven that I am thus and thus;
And that which we profanely term our fortunes
Is the provision of the power above,
Fitted and shaped just to that strength of nature
Which we are borne withal. Good God, good God,
That I from such an humble bench of birth
Should step as 'twere up to my country's head
And give the law out there; ay, in my father's life,
To take prerogative and tithe of knees
From elder kinsmen, and him bind by my place
To give the smooth and dexter way to me
That owe it him by nature. Sure, these things,
Not physicked by respect, might turn our blood
To much corruption. But More, the more thou hast,
Either of honour, office, wealth, and calling,
Which might excite thee to embrace and hug them,
The more do thou in serpents' natures think them,
Fear their gay skins with thought of their sharp state,
And let this be thy maxim: to be great
Is when the thread of hazard is once spun,
A bottom great wound up, greatly undone.
Come on, sir: are you ready?

Enter Randall, attired like Sir Thomas More.

Randall   Yes, my lord, I stand but on a few points. I shall have
done presently. Before God, I have practised your
lordship's shift so well that I think I shall grow
proud, my lord.

More   'Tis fit thou shouldst wax proud, or else thou'lt ne'er
Be near allied to greatness. Observe me, sirrah:

The learnèd clerk Erasmus is arrived
Within our English court. Last night I hear
He feasted with our honoured English poet,
The Earl of Surrey; and I learned today
The famous clerk of Rotterdam will visit
Sir Thomas More. Therefore, sir, take my seat:
You are lord chancellor. Dress your behaviour
According to my carriage, but beware
You talk not over much, for 'twill betray thee.
Who prates not much seems wise, his wit few scan,
While the tongue blabs tales of the imperfect man.
I'll see if great Erasmus can distinguish
Merit and outward ceremony.

Randall	If I do not serve a share for playing of your lordship well, let me be yeoman usher to your sumpter and be banished from wearing of a gold chain forever.
More	Well, sir, I'll hide our motion; act thy part With a firm boldness, and thou winst my heart.

Enter the Sheriff with Faulkner, a ruffian, and Officers.

	How now? What's the matter?
Faulkner	Tug me not, I'm no bear. 'Sblood, if all the dogs in Paris Garden hung at my tail, I'd shake 'em off with this: that I'll appear before no king christened but my good lord chancellor.
Sheriff	We'll christen you, sirrah. Bring him forward.
More	How now, what tumults make you?
Faulkner	The azured heavens protect my noble lord chancellor.
More	What fellow's this?
Sheriff	A ruffian, my lord, that hath set half the city in an uproar.
Faulkner	My lord –
Sheriff	There was a fray in Paternoster Row, and because they would not be parted, the street was choked up with carts.

Faulkner	My noble lord, Panyer Alley's throat was open.
More	Sirrah, hold your peace.
Faulkner	I'll prove the street was not choked, but is as well as ever it was since it was a street.
Sheriff	This fellow was a principal broacher of the broil –
Faulkner	'Sblood, I broached none; it was broached and half run out before I had a lick at it.
Sheriff	And would be brought before no justice but your honour.
Faulkner	I am haled, my noble lord.
More	No ear to choose for every trivial noise But mine, and in so full a time? Away, You wrong me, master shrieve. Dispose of him At your own pleasure; send the knave to Newgate.
Faulkner	To Newgate? 'Sblood, Sir Thomas More, I appeal, I appeal! From Newgate to any of the two worshipful Counters.
More	Fellow, whose man are you, that are thus lusty?
Faulkner	My name's Jack Faulkner. I serve, next under God and my prince, Master Morris, secretary to my Lord of Winchester.
More	A fellow of your hair is very fit To be a secretary's follower.
Faulkner	I hope so, my lord. The fray was between the Bishops' men of Ely and Winchester; and I could not in honour but part them. I thought it stood not with my reputation and degree to come to my questions and answers before a city justice: I knew I should to the pot.
More	Thou hast been there, it seems, too late already.
Faulkner	I know your honour is wise and so forth; and I desire to be only catechised or examined by you, my noble lord chancellor.

More	Sirrah, sirrah, you are a busy dangerous ruffian.
Faulkner	Ruffian?
More	How long have you worn this hair?
Faulkner	I have worn this hair ever since I was born.
More	You know that's not my question, but how long Hath this shag fleece hung dangling on thy head?
Faulkner	How long, my lord? Why, sometimes thus long, sometimes lower, as the Fates and humours please.
More	So quick, sir, with me, ha? I see, good fellow, Thou lovest plain dealing. Sirrah, tell me now, When were you last at barber's? How long time Have you upon your head worn this shag hair?
Faulkner	My lord, Jack Faulkner tells no Aesop's fables: troth, I was not at barber's this three years; I have not been cut nor will not be cut, upon a foolish vow, which, as the destinies shall direct I am sworn to keep.
More	When comes that vow out?
Faulkner	Why, when the humours are purged: not this three years.
More	Vows are recorded in the court of heaven, For they are holy acts. Young man, I charge thee And do advise thee, start not from that vow; And for I will be sure thou shalt not shrive, Besides, because it is an odious sight To see a man thus hairy, thou shalt lie In Newgate till thy vow and thy three years Be full expired. Away with him.
Faulkner	My lord –
More	Cut off this fleece, and lie there but a month.
Faulkner	I'll not lose a hair to be lord chancellor of Europe.
More	To Newgate, then. Sirrah, great sins are bred In all that body where there's a foul head. Away with him.

Exeunt all except Randall.

Enter Surrey, Erasmus, and Attendants.

Surrey   Now, great Erasmus, you approach the presence
Of a most worthy learnèd gentleman.
This little isle holds not a truer friend
Unto the arts, nor doth his greatness add
A feignèd flourish to his worthy parts:
He's great in study; that's the statist's grace,
That gains more reverence than the outward place.

Erasmus   Report, my lord, hath crossed the narrow seas
And to the several parts of christendom
Hath borne the fame of your lord chancellor.
I long to see him whom with loving thoughts
I in my study oft have visited.
Is that Sir Thomas More?

Surrey   It is, Erasmus.
Now shall you view the honourablest scholar,
The most religious politician,
The worthiest counsellor that tends our state.
That study is the general watch of England:
In it the prince's safety, and the peace
That shines upon our commonwealth are forged
By loyal industry.

Erasmus   I doubt him not
To be as near the life of excellence
As you proclaim him, when his meanest servants
Are of some weight. You saw, my lord, his porter
Give entertainment to us at the gate
In Latin good phrase. What's the master then,
When such good parts shine in his meanest men?

Surrey   His lordship hath some weighty business,
For see, as yet he takes no notice of us.

Erasmus   I think 'twere best I did my duty to him
In a short Latin speech. –
Qui in celiberrima patria natus est et gloriosa plus habet
negotii ut in lucem veniat quam qui –

Randall	I prithee thee, good Erasmus, be covered. I have forsworn speaking of Latin, else as I am true counsellor, I'd tickle you with a speech. Nay sit, Erasmus; sit, good my Lord of Surrey. I'll make my lady come to you anon, if she will, and give you entertainment.
Erasmus	Is this Sir Thomas More?
Surrey	O good Erasmus, you must conceive his vein: He's ever furnished with these conceits.
Randall	Yes faith, my learned poet doth not lie for that matter: I am neither more nor less than merry Sir Thomas always. Wilt sup with me? By God, I love a parlous wise fellow that smells of a politician better than a long progress.

Enter Sir Thomas More.

Surrey	We are deluded; this is not his lordship.
Randall	I pray you, Erasmus, how long will the Holland cheese in your country keep without maggots?
More	Fool, painted barbarism, retire thyself Into thy first creation!

Exit Randall.

Thus you see,
My loving learnèd friends, how far respect
Waits often on the ceremonious train
Of base illiterate wealth, whilst men of schools,
Shrouded in poverty, are counted fools.
Pardon, thou reverent German, I have mixed
So slight a jest to the fair entertainment
Of thy most worthy self; for know, Erasmus,
Mirth wrinkles up my face, and I still crave
When that forsakes me I may hug my grave.

Erasmus	Your honour's merry humour is best physic Unto your able body. For we learn Where melancholy chokes the passages Of blood and breath, the erected spirit still Lengthens our days with sportful exercise.

Study should be the saddest time of life,
The rest a sport exempt from thought of strife.

More   Erasmus preacheth gospel against physic,
My noble poet –

Surrey   O, my lord, you tax me
In that word poet of much idleness.
It is a study that makes poor our fate:
Poets were ever thought unfit for state.

More   O, give not up fair poesy, sweet lord,
To such contempt. That I may speak my heart,
It is the sweetest heraldry of art
That sets a difference 'tween the tough sharp holly
And tender bay tree.

Surrey   Yet, my lord,
It is become the very lag number
To all mechanic sciences.

More   Why, I'll show the reason:
This is no age for poets; they should sing
To the loud canon *heroica facta;*
Qui faciunt reges heroica carmina laudant:
And as great subjects of their pen decay,
Even so unphysicked they do melt away.

Enter Master Morris.

Come, will your lordship in? My dear Erasmus –
I'll hear you, Master Morris, presently. –
My lord, I make you master of my house;
We'll banquet here with fresh and staid delights,
The Muses' music here shall cheer our sprites;
The cates must be but mean where scholars sit,
For they're made all with courses of neat wit.

Exeunt Surrey, Erasmus, and Attendants.

How now, Master Morris?

Morris   I am a suitor to your lordship in behalf of a servant
of mine.

More   The fellow with long hair? Good Master Morris,
Come to me three years hence and then I'll hear you.

Morris	I understand your honour, but the foolish knave has submitted himself to the mercy of a barber, and is without, ready to make a new vow before your lordship hereafter to live civil.
More	Nay, then, let's talk with him; pray, call him in.

Enter Faulkner and Officers.

Faulkner	Bless your honour, a new man, my lord.
More	Why, sure, this is not he.
Faulkner	And your lordship will, the barber shall give you a sample of my head. I am he in faith, my lord; I am *ipse*.
More	Why, now thy face is like an honest man's. Thou hast played well at this new cut and won.
Faulkner	No, my lord, lost all that ever God sent me.
More	God sent thee into the world as thou art now, With a short hair. How quickly are three years Run out of Newgate.
Faulkner	I think so, my lord; for there was but a hair's length between my going thither and so long time.
More	Because I see some grace in thee, go free. Discharge him, fellows. Farewell, Master Morris. Thy head is for thy shoulders now more fit: Thou hast less hair upon it, but more wit. *Exit.*
Morris	Did not I tell thee always of these locks?
Faulkner	And the locks were on again, all the goldsmiths in Cheapside should not pick them open. 'Sheart, if my hair stand not on end when I look for my face in a glass, I am a polecat. Here's a lousy jest. But if I notch not that rogue Tom barber that makes me look thus like a Brownist, hang me. I'll be worse to the nittical knave than ten tooth drawings. Here's a head with a pox!
Morris	What ailst thou? Art thou mad now?

Faulkner	Mad now? 'Nails, if loss of hair cannot mad a man, what can? I am deposed, my crown is taken from me. More had been better a scoured Moorditch than 'a notched me thus. Does he begin sheep-shearing with Jack Faulkner?
Morris	Nay, and you feed this vein sir, fare you well.
Faulkner	Why, farewell frost. I'll go hang myself out for the poll head. Make a Sar'cen of Jack?
Morris	Thou desperate knave, for that I see the devil Wholly gets hold of thee –
Faulkner	The devil's a damned rascal.
Morris	I charge thee wait on me no more, no more Call me thy master.
Faulkner	Why then, a word Master Morris.
Morris	I'll hear no words, sir; fare you well.
Faulkner	'Sblood, farewell?
Morris	Why dost thou follow me?
Faulkner	Because I'm an ass. Do you set your shavers upon me, and then cast me off? Must I condole? Have the fates played the fools? Am I their cut? Now the poor sconce is taken, must Jack march with bag and baggage? *Weeps.*
Morris	You coxcomb.
Faulkner	Nay, you ha' poached me; you ha' given me a hair; it's here, here.
Morris	Away, you kind ass. Come, sir, dry your eyes; Keep your old place, and mend these fooleries.
Faulkner	I care not to be turned off, and 'twere a ladder, so it be in my humour, or the fates beckon to me. Nay pray sir, if the destinies spin me a fine thread, Faulkner flies another pitch; and to avoid the headache hereafter, before I'll be a hairmonger I'll be a whoremonger.

Exeunt.

SCENE TWO

Enter Sir Thomas More and a Messenger to More.

Messenger   My honourable lord, the mayor of London,
            Accompanied with his lady and her train,
            Are coming hither, and are hard at hand,
            To feast with you. A servant's come before
            To tell your lordship of their near approach.

More   Why, this is cheerful news. Friends go and come:
            Reverend Erasmus, whose delicious words
            Express the very soul and life of wit,
            Newly took sad leave of me, and with tears
            Troubled the silver channel of the Thames,
            Which, glad of such a burden, proudly swelled
            And on her bosom bore him toward the sea.
            He's gone to Rotterdam; peace go with him.
            He left me heavy when he went from hence,
            But this recomforts me: the kind lord mayor,
            His brethren aldermen with their fair wives,
            Will feast this night with us. Why, so 't should be:
            More's merry heart lives by good company.
            Good gentlemen, be careful; give great charge
            Our diet be made dainty for the taste,
            For of all people that the earth affords,
            The Londoners fare richest at their boards.

                                                Exeunt.

SCENE THREE

*Enter Sir Thomas More, Master Roper, and Servingmen
setting stools.*

More   Come, my good fellows, stir, be diligent,
            Sloth is an idle fellow, leave him now;
            The time requires your expeditious service.
            Place me here stools to set the ladies on.
            Son Roper, you have given order for the banquet?

Roper	I have, my lord, and everything is ready.

Enter Lady More.

More	O, welcome, wife. Give you direction
	How women should be placed, you know it best.
	For my lord mayor, his brethren, and the rest,
	Let me alone: men best can order men.
Lady More	I warrant ye, my lord, all shall be well.
	There's one without that stays to speak with ye,
	And bade me tell ye that he is a player.
More	A player, wife? One of ye bid him come in.

Exit Servingman.

Nay, stir there fellows, fie, ye are too slow.
See that your lights be in a readiness,
The banquet shall be here. God's me, madam,
Leave my lady mayoress? Both of us from the board?
And my son Roper too? What may our guests think?

Lady More	My lord, they are risen and sitting by the fire.
More	Why, yet go you and keep them company;
	It is not meet we should be absent both.

Exit Lady.

Enter Player.

Welcome good friend; what is your will with me?

Player	My lord, my fellows and myself
	Are come to tender ye our willing service,
	So please you to command us.
More	What, for a play, you mean?
	Whom do you serve?
Player	My lord Cardinal's grace.
More	My lord Cardinal's players? Now trust me, welcome.
	You happen hither in a lucky time,
	To pleasure me, and benefit yourselves.
	The mayor of London and some aldermen,
	His lady and their wives, are my kind guests

This night at supper. Now, to have a play
Before the banquet will be excellent.
How think you, son Roper?

Roper   'Twill do well, my lord,
And be right pleasing pastime to your guests.

More   I prithee tell me, what plays have ye?

Player   Diverse, my lord: *The Cradle of Security*,
Hit Nail o' the Head, *Impatient Poverty*,
The Play of Four P's, *Dives and Lazarus*,
Lusty Juventus, and *The Marriage of Wit and Wisdom*.

More   *The Marriage of Wit and Wisdom*? That, my lads,
I'll none but that; the theme is very good,
And may maintain a liberal argument.
To marry wit to wisdom asks some cunning:
Many have wit that may come short of wisdom.
We'll see how master poet plays his part,
And whether wit or wisdom grace his art.
Go, make him drink, and all his fellows too.
How many are ye?

Player   Four men and a boy, sir.

More   But one boy? Then I see
There's but few women in the play.

Player   Three, my lord: Dame Science, Lady Vanity,
And Wisdom, she herself.

More   And one boy play them all? By our Lady, he's laden.
Well, my good fellow, get ye straight together,
And make ye ready with what haste ye may.
Provide their supper 'gainst the play be done,
Else shall we stay our guests here over long.
Make haste, I pray ye.

Player   We will, my lord.

                              Exeunt Servingman and Player.

More   Where are the waits? Go, bid them play,
To spend the time a while.

Enter Lady.

How now, madam?

Lady More My lord, th' are coming hither.

More Th' are welcome. Wife, I'll tell ye one thing:
Our sport is somewhat mended; we shall have
A play tonight, *The Marriage of Wit and Wisdom*,
And acted by my good lord Cardinal's players.
How like ye that, wife?

Lady More My lord, I like it well.
See, they are coming.

*Enter Lord Mayor, so many Aldermen as may, the Lady Mayoress
in scarlet, with other Ladies and Sir Thomas More's Daughters;
Servants carrying lighted torches by them.*

More Once again, welcome, welcome my good lord mayor,
And brethren all, for once I was your brother
And so I am still in heart. It is not state
That can our love from London separate.
True, upstart fools, by sudden fortune tried,
Regard their former mates with naught but pride.
But they that cast an eye still whence they came,
Know how they rose, and how to use the same.

Lord Mayor My lord, you set a gloss on London's fame,
And make it happy ever by your name.
Needs must we say, when we remember More,
'Twas he that drove rebellion from our door
With grave discretion's mild and gentle breath
Shielding a many subjects' lives from death.
O how our city is by you renowned,
And with your virtues our endeavours crowned.

More No more, my good lord mayor; but thanks to all
That on so short a summons you would come
To visit him that holds your kindness dear.
Madam, you are not merry with my lady mayoress
And these fair ladies; pray ye, seat them all,
And here, my lord, let me appoint your place –
The rest to seat themselves. Nay, I'll weary ye:
You will not long in haste to visit me.

Lady More Good madam, sit; in sooth, you shall sit here.

Lady Mayoress Good madam, pardon me, it may not be.

Lady More In troth, I'll have it so: I'll sit here by ye.
Good ladies, sit. More stools here, ho!

Lady Mayoress It is your favour, madam, makes me thus
Presume above my merit.

Lady More   When we come to you,
Then shall you rule us as we rule you here.
Now must I tell ye, madam, we have a play
To welcome ye withal; how good soe'er
That know not I; my lord will have it so.

More Wife, hope the best; I am sure they'll do their best;
They that would better comes not at their feast.
My good lord Cardinal's players, I thank them for it,
Play us a play, to lengthen out your welcome.
They say it is *The Marriage of Wit and Wisdom*,
A theme of some import, howe'er it prove;
But if art fail, we'll inch it out with love.

Enter a Servant.

What, are they ready?

Servant My lord, one of the players craves to speak with you.

More With me? Where is he?

Enter Inclination, the Vice, ready.

Inclination Here, my lord.

More How now, what's the matter?

Inclination We would desire your honour but to stay a little: one
of my fellows is but run to Ogle's for a long beard
for young Wit, and he'll be here presently.

More A long beard for young Wit? Why, man, he may be
without a beard till he come to marriage, for wit goes
not all by the hair. When comes Wit in?

Inclination In the second scene, next to the prologue, my lord.

More	Why, play on till that scene come, and by that time Wit's beard will be grown, or else the fellow returned with it. And what part playst thou?
Inclination	Inclination the Vice, my lord.
More	Gramercies, now I may take the vice if I list; and wherefore hast thou that bridle in thy hand?
Inclination	I must be bridled anon, my lord.
More	And thou beest not saddled too, it makes no matter, for then Wit's inclination may gallop so fast, that he will outstrip wisdom and fall to folly.
Inclination	Indeed, so he does to Lady Vanity; but we have no Folly in our play.
More	Then there's no wit in 't, I'll be sworn: folly waits on wit as the shadow on the body, and where wit is ripest, there folly still is readiest. But begin, I prithee; we'll rather allow a beardless Wit, than wit all beard to have no brain.
Inclination	Nay, he has his apparel on too, my lord, and therefore he is the readier to enter.
More	Then, good Inclination, begin at a venture.

Exit Inclination.

My lord mayor,
Wit lacks a beard, or else they would begin.
I'd lend him mine, but that it is too thin.
Silence, they come.   *The trumpet sounds.*

Enter the Prologue.

Prologue	Now for as much as in these latter days Throughout the whole world in every land Vice doth increase and virtue decays, Iniquity having the upper hand; We therefore intend, good gentle audience, A pretty short interlude to play at this present, Desiring your leave and quiet silence, To show the same, as is meet and expedient. It is called *The Marriage of Wit and Wisdom*.

A matter right pithy and pleasing to hear,
Whereof in brief we will show the whole sum.
But I must be gone, for Wit doth appear.   *Exit.*

Enter Wit, ruffling, and Inclination the Vice.

Wit   In an arbour green, asleep whereas I lay,
              The birds sang sweetly in the midst of the day,
              I dreamed fast of mirth and play.
              In youth is pleasure, in youth is pleasure,
              Methought I walked still to and fro,
              And from her company I could not go,
              But when I waked, it was not so.
              In youth is pleasure, in youth is pleasure.
              Therefore my heart is surely plight,
              Of her alone to have a sight,
              Which is my joy and heart's delight.
              In youth is pleasure, in youth is pleasure.

More   Mark ye, my lord, this is Wit without a beard; what
              will he be by that time he comes to the commodity
              of a beard?

Inclination   O sir, the ground is the better on which she doth go.
              For she will make better cheer with a little she can get,
              Than many a one can with a great banquet of meat.

Wit   And is her name Wisdom?

Inclination   Ay, sir, a wife most fit
              For you, my good master, my dainty sweet Wit.

Wit   To be in her company my heart it is set.
              Therefore I prithee to let us be gone,
              For unto Wisdom Wit hath inclination.

Inclination   O sir, she will come herself even anon,
              For I told her before where we would stand,
              And then she said she would beck us with her hand.
              Back with these boys and saucy great knaves!

                                    Flourishing his dagger.

              What, stand ye here so big in your braves?
              My dagger about your coxcombs shall walk
              If I may but so much as hear ye chat or talk.

Wit	But will she take pains to come for us hither?
Inclination	I warrant ye, therefore you must be familiar with her;
	When she commeth in place,
	You must her embrace
	Somewhat handsomely,
	Lest she think it danger,
	Because you are a stranger,
	To come in your company.
Wit	I warrant thee, Inclination, I will be busy.
	O how Wit longs to be in Wisdom's company!

Enter Lady Vanity singing, and beckoning with her hand.

Vanity	Come hither, come hither, come hither, come:
	Such cheer as I have, thou shalt have some.
More	This is Lady Vanity, I'll hold my life:
	Beware, good Wit, you take not her to wife.
Inclination	What, Unknown Honesty, word in your ear.

She offers to depart.

	You shall not be gone as yet, I swear:
	Here's none but friends, you need not to fray;
	This young gentleman loves ye, therefore you must
	stay.
Wit	I trust in me she will think no danger,
	For I love well the company of fair women;
	And though to you I am a stranger,
	Yet Wit may pleasure you now and then.
Vanity	Who, you? Nay, you are such a holy man,
	That to touch one you dare not be bold.
	I think you would not kiss a young woman
	If one would give ye twenty pound in gold.
Wit	Yes, in good sadness, lady, that I would;
	I could find in my heart to kiss you in your smock.
Vanity	My back is broad enough to bear that mock.
	For it hath been told me many a time
	That you would be seen in no such company as mine.

Wit	Not Wit in the company of Lady Wisdom?
	O Jove, for what do I hither come?
Inclination	Sir, she did this nothing else but to prove
	Whether a little thing would you move
	To be angry and fret.
	What, and if one said so,
	Let such trifling matters go
	And with a kind kiss come out of her debt. –
	Is Luggins come yet with the beard?

Enter another Player.

Player	No, faith, he is not come. Alas, what shall we do?
Inclination	Forsooth, we can go no further till our fellow
	Luggins come; for he plays Good Counsel, and now
	he should enter to admonish Wit that this is Lady
	Vanity and not Lady Wisdom.
More	Nay, and it be no more but so, ye shall not tarry at
	a stand for that; we'll not have our play marred for
	lack of a little good counsel: till your fellow come,
	I'll give him the best counsel that I can. Pardon me,
	my lord mayor, I love to be merry.
	O Wit, thou art now on the bow hand,
	And blindly in thine own opinion dost stand.
	I tell thee, this naughty lewd Inclination
	Does lead thee amiss in a very strange fashion.
	This is not Wisdom, but Lady Vanity;
	Therefore list to Good Counsel, and be ruled by me.
Inclination	In troth, my lord, it is as right to Luggins's part as
	can be. Speak, Wit.
More	Nay, we will not have our audience disappointed, if I
	can help it.
Wit	Art thou Good Counsel, and will tell me so?
	Wouldst thou have Wit from Lady Wisdom to go?
	Thou art some deceiver, I tell thee verily,
	In saying that this is Lady Vanity.
More	Wit, judge not things by the outward show:
	The eye oft mistakes, right well you do know.

Good Counsel assures thee upon his honesty
That this is not Wisdom, but Lady Vanity.

Enter Luggins with the beard.

Inclination   O my lord, he is come; now we shall go forward.

More   Art thou come? Well, fellow, I have help to save
thine honesty a little. Now, if thou canst give Wit
any better counsel than I have done, spare not.
There I leave him to thy mercy.
But by this time, I am sure, our banquet's ready:
My lord and ladies, we will taste that first
And then they shall begin the play again,
Which, through the fellow's absence, and by me,
Instead of helping, hath been hindered.
Prepare against we come. Lights there, I say.
Thus fools oft times do help to mar the play.

Exeunt all but the Players.

Wit   Fie, fellow Luggins, you serve us handsomely, do ye
not, think ye?

Luggins   Why, Ogle was not within, and his wife would not
let me have the beard, and, by my troth, I ran so fast
that I sweat again.

Inclination   Do ye hear, fellows? Would not my lord make a rare
player? O, he would uphold a company beyond all
hope, better than Mason among the King's players!
Did ye mark how extemprically he fell to the matter,
and spake Luggins's part almost as it is in the very
book set down?

Wit   Peace, do ye know what ye say? My lord a player?
Let us not meddle with any such matters. Yet I may
be a little proud that my lord hath answered me in
my part. But come, let us go, and be ready to begin
the play again.

Luggins   Ay, that's the best, for now we lack nothing.

Enter a Servingman.

Servingman   Where be these players?

All	Here, sir.

Servingman My lord is sent for to the court,
        And all the guests do after supper part;
        And for he will not trouble you again,
        By me for your reward 'a sends eight angels
        With many thanks. But sup before you go:
        It is his will you should be fairly entreated.
        Follow, I pray ye.

Wit   This, Luggins, is your negligence:
        Wanting Wit's beard brought things into dislike,
        For otherwise the play had been all seen,
        Where now some curious citizen disgraced it
        And, discommending it, all is dismissed.

Inclination 'Fore God, 'a says true. But hear ye, sirs: eight angels,
        ha? My lord would never give eight angels; more or
        less for twelvepence. Either it should be three pounds,
        five pounds, or ten pounds. There's twenty shillings
        wanting, sure.

Wit   Twenty to one 'tis so. I have a trick. – My lord
        comes; stand aside.

        Enter More with Attendants with Purse and Mace.

More   In haste to council! What's the business now,
        That all so late his highness sends for me? –
        What seekst thou, fellow?

Wit   Nay, nothing.
        Your lordship sent eight angels by your man,
        And I have lost two of them in the rushes.

More   Wit, look to that. Eight angels? I did send
        Them ten. Who gave it them?

Servingman I, my lord; I had no more about me;
        But by and by they shall receive the rest.

More   Well, Wit, 'twas wisely done; thou playest Wit well
        indeed,
        Not to be thus deceivèd of thy right.
        Am I a man, by office truly ordained

Equally to divide true right his own,
And shall I have deceivers in my house?
Then what avails my bounty, when such servants
Deceive the poor of what the master gives?
Go one, and pull his coat over his ears.
There are too many such. Give them their right.
Wit, let thy fellows thank thee: 'twas well done;
Thou now deservest to match with Lady Wisdom.

Exit More with Attendants.

Inclination   God a' mercy, Wit. Sir, you had a master Sir Thomas
More more; but now we shall have more.

Luggins   God bless him. I would there were more of his
mind: 'a loves our quality; and yet he's a learned
man, and knows what the world is.

Player   Well, a kind man, and more loving than many other,
but I think we ha' met with the first –

Luggins   First served his man that had our angels; and he may
chance dine with Duke Humphrey tomorrow, being
turned away today. Come, let's go.

Player   And many such rewards would make us all ride and
horse us with the best nags in Smithfield.

Exeunt.

ACT FOUR

SCENE ONE

*Enter the Earls of Shrewsbury, Surrey, Bishop of Rochester,
and other Lords; severally, doing courtesy to each other;
Clerk of the Council waiting bareheaded.*

Surrey	Good morrow to my lord of Shrewsbury.
Shrewsbury	The like unto the honoured Earl of Surrey.
	Yond comes my lord of Rochester.
Rochester	Good morrow, my good lords.
Surrey	Clerk of the Council, what time is't of day?
Clerk	Past eight of clock, my lord.
Shrewsbury	I wonder that my good lord chancellor
	Doth stay so long, considering there's matters
	Of high importance to be scanned upon.
Surrey	Clerk of the Council, certify his lordship
	The lords expect him here.
Rochester	It shall not need:
	Yond comes his lordship.

Enter Sir Thomas More, with Purse and Mace borne before him.

More	Good morrow to this fair assembly.
	Come, my good lords, let's sit. O serious square,

They sit.

Upon this little board is daily scanned
The health and preservation of the land.
We the physicians that effect this good,
Now by choice diet, anon by letting blood.
Our toil and careful watching brings the king
In league with slumbers, to which peace doth sing.
Avoid the room there. –
What business, lords, today?

Shrewsbury   This, my good lord;
          About the entertainment of the emperor
          'Gainst the perfidious French into our pay.

Surrey   My lords, as 'tis the custom in this place
          The youngest should speak first, so if I chance
          In this case to speak youngly, pardon me.
          I will agree, France now hath her full strength,
          As having new recovered the pale blood
          Which war sluiced forth, and I consent to this,
          That the conjunction of our English forces
          With arms of Germany may sooner bring
          This prize of conquest in. But then, my lords,
          As in the moral hunting 'twixt the lion
          And other beasts, force joined with guile
          Frighted the weaker sharers from their parts,
          So if the empire's sovereign chance to put
          His plea of partnership into war's court,
          Swords should decide the difference, and our blood
          In private tears lament his entertainment.

Shrewsbury To doubt the worst is still the wise man's shield,
          That arms him safely: but the world knows this,
          The emperor is a man of royal faith;
          His love unto our sovereign brings him down
          From his imperial seat, to march in pay
          Under our English flag, and wear the cross
          Like some high order on his manly breast.
          Thus serving, he's not master of himself,
          But like a colonel, commanding other,
          Is by the general over-awed himself.

Rochester Yet, my good lord –

Shrewsbury   Let me conclude my speech.
          As subjects share no portion in the conquest
          Of their true sovereign, other than the merit
          That from the sovereign guerdons the true subject,
          So the good emperor, in a friendly league
          Of amity with England, will not soil
          His honour with the theft of English spoil.

More	There is no question but this entertainment
	Will be most honourable, most commodious.
	I have oft heard good captains wish to have
	Rich soldiers to attend them, such as would fight
	Both for their lives and livings. Such a one
	Is the good emperor: I would to God,
	We had ten thousand of such able men.
	Ha, then there would appear no court, no city,
	But, where the wars were: they would pay themselves.
	Then to prevent in French wars England's loss,
	Let German flags wave with our English cross.

Enter Sir Thomas Palmer.

Palmer	My lords, his majesty hath sent by me
	These articles enclosed, first to be viewed,
	And then to be subscribed to. I tender them
	In that due reverence which befits this place.

With great reverence.

More	Subscribe these articles? Stay, let us pause:
	Our conscience first shall parley with our laws.
	My Lord of Rochester, view you the paper.

Rochester	Subscribe to these? Now good Sir Thomas Palmer,
	Beseech the king that he will pardon me.
	My heart will check my hand whilst I do write:
	Subscribing so, I were an hypocrite.

Palmer	Do you refuse it then, my lord?

Rochester	I do, Sir Thomas.

Palmer	Then here I summon you forthwith t' appear
	Before his majesty, to answer there
	This capital contempt.

Rochester	I rise and part,
	In lieu of this, to tender him my heart.

He riseth.

Palmer	Will't please your honour to subscribe, my lord?

More	Sir, tell his highness I entreat Some time for to bethink me of this task. In the meanwhile I do resign mine office Into my sovereign's hands.
Palmer	Then, my lord, Hear the preparèd order from the king: On your refusal, you shall straight depart Unto your house at Chelsea, till you know Our sovereign's further pleasure.
More	Most willingly I go. My lords, if you will visit me at Chelsea, We'll go a-fishing, and with a cunning net, Not like weak film, we'll catch none but the great. Farewell, my noble lords. Why, this is right: Good morrow to the sun, to state good night.

Exit More.

Palmer	Will you subscribe, my lords?
Surrey	Instantly, good Sir Thomas, We'll bring the writing unto our sovereign.

They write.

Palmer	My Lord of Rochester, You must with me, to answer this contempt.
Rochester	This is the worst, Who's freed from life is from all care exempt.

Exeunt Rochester and Palmer.

Surrey	Now let us hasten to our sovereign. 'Tis strange that my Lord Chancellor should refuse The duty that the law of God bequeaths Unto the king.
Shrewsbury	Come, let us in. No doubt His mind will alter, and the bishop's too. Error in learned heads hath much to do.

Exeunt.

SCENE TWO

Enter the Lady More, her two Daughters,
and Master Roper, as walking.

Roper   Madam, what ails ye for to look so sad?

Lady More   Troth, son, I know not what, I am not sick,
            And yet I am not well: I would be merry,
            But somewhat lies so heavy on heart,
            I cannot choose but sigh. You are a scholar:
            I pray ye tell me, may one credit dreams?

Roper   Why ask you that, dear madam?

Lady More   Because tonight I had the strangest dream
            That e'er my sleep was troubled with.
            Methought 'twas night,
            And that the king and queen went on the Thames
            In barges to hear music. My lord and I
            Were in a little boat methought, – Lord, Lord,
            What strange things live in slumbers! – and, being
                                                          near,
            We grappled to the barge that bare the king.
            But after many pleasing voices spent
            In that still moving music house, methought
            The violence of the stream did sever us
            Quite from the golden fleet, and hurried us
            Unto the bridge, which with unusèd horror
            We entered at full tide; thence some slight shoot
            Being carried by the waves, our boat stood still
            Just opposite the Tower, and there it turned
            And turned about, as when a whirlpool sucks
            The circled waters. Methought that we both cried,
            Till that we sunk, where arm in arm we died.

Roper   Give no respect, dear madam, to fond dreams.
            They are but slight illusions of the blood.

Lady More   Tell me not all are so, for often dreams
            Are true diviners, either of good or ill.
            I cannot be in quiet till I hear
            How my lord fares.

Roper	(*Aside*) Nor I. – Come hither, wife,
	I will not fright thy mother to interpret
	The nature of a dream; but trust me, sweet,
	This night I have been troubled with thy father
	Beyond all thought.

Roper's Wife	Truly, and so have I:
	Methought I saw him here in Chelsea Church,
	Standing upon the rood loft, now defac'd,
	And whilst he kneeled and prayed before the image,
	It fell with him into the upper choir,
	Where my poor father lay all stained in blood.

Roper	Our dreams all meet in one conclusion,
	Fatal, I fear.

Lady More	What's that you talk? I pray ye, let me know it.

Roper's Wife	Nothing, good mother.

Lady More	This is your fashion still; I must know nothing.
	Call Master Catesby; he shall straight to court,
	And see how my lord does: I shall not rest
	Until my heart leave panting on his breast.

Enter Sir Thomas More merrily, Servants attending.

Daughter	See where my father comes, joyful and merry.

More	As seamen, having passed a troubled storm,
	Dance on the pleasant shore, so I – O, I could speak
	Now like a poet. Now afore God I am passing light.
	Wife, give me kind welcome; thou wast wont to
	blame
	My kissing, when my beard was in the stubble,
	But I have been trimmed of late, I have had
	A smooth court shaving, in good faith I have.

Daughters kneel.

	God bless ye. Son Roper, give me your hand.

Roper	Your honour's welcome home.

More	Honour? Ha ha.
	And how dost, wife?

Roper	He bears himself most strangely.

Lady More	Will your lordship in?
More	Lordship? No, wife, that's gone,
	The ground was slight that we did lean upon.
Lady More	Lord, that your honour ne'er will leave these jests.
	In faith, it ill becomes ye.
More	O, good wife,
	Honour and jests are both together fled;
	The merriest councillor of England's dead.
Lady More	Who's that, my lord?
More	Still lord? The lord chancellor, wife.
Lady More	That's you.
More	Certain, but I have changed my life.
	Am I not leaner than I was before?
	The fat is gone: my title's only More.
	Contented with one style, I'll live at rest:
	They that have many names are not still best.
	I have resigned mine office: countst me not wise?
Lady More	O God.
More	Come, breed not female children in your eyes.
	The king will have it so.
Lady More	What's the offence?
More	Tush, let that pass, we'll talk of that anon.
	The king seems a physician to my fate,
	His princely mind would train me back to state.
Roper	Then be his patient, my most honoured father.
More	O, son Roper,
	Ubi turpis est medicina, sanari piget! –
	No, wife, be merry, and be merry all,
	You smiled at rising, weep not at my fall.
	Let's in, and here joy like to private friends,
	Since days of pleasure have repentant ends.
	The light of greatness is with triumph borne:
	It sets at midday oft, with public scorn.

Exeunt.

SCENE THREE

Enter the Bishop of Rochester, Surrey, Shrewsbury,
Lieutenant of the Tower, and Warders with weapons.

Rochester   Your kind persuasions, honourable lords,
              I can but thank ye for, but in this breast
              There lives a soul, that aims at higher things
              Than temporary pleasing earthly kings.
              God bless his highness even with all my heart,
              We shall meet one day, though that now we part.

Surrey   We not misdoubt, your wisdom can discern
              What best befits it; yet in love and zeal
              We could entreat, it might be otherwise.

Shrewsbury   No doubt your fatherhood will by yourself
              Consider better of the present case,
              And grow as great in favour as before.

Rochester   For that, as pleaseth God. In my restraint
              From wordly causes, I shall better see
              Into myself than at proud liberty.
              The Tower and I will privately confer
              Of things, wherein at freedom I may err.
              But I am troublesome unto your honours,
              And hold ye longer than becomes my duty.
              Master Lieutenant, I am now your charge,
              And though you keep my body, yet my love
              Waits on my king and you, while Fisher lives.

Surrey   Farewell my Lord of Rochester, we'll pray
              For your release, and labour't as we may.

Shrewsbury   Thereof assure yourself. So do we leave ye,
              And to your happy private thoughts bequeath ye.

Exeunt Lords.

Rochester   Now, Master Lieutenant, on, a God's name go,
              And with as glad a mind go I with you
              As ever truant bade the school adieu.

Exeunt.

SCENE FOUR

Enter Sir Thomas More, his Lady, Daughters, Master Roper,
Gentlemen, and Servants, as in his house at Chelsea.

More   Good morrow, good son Roper; sit, good madam,
                                      Low stools.
        Upon an humble seat: the time so craves.
        Rest your good heart on earth, the roof of graves.
        You see the floor of greatness is uneven,
        The cricket and high throne alike near heaven.
        Now daughters, you that like to branches spread
        And give best shadow to a private house,
        Be comforted, my girls, your hopes stand fair:
        Virtue breeds gentry, she makes the best heir.

Both Daughters   Good morrow to your honour.

More   Nay, good night rather.
        Your honour's crestfall'n with your happy father.

Roper   O, what formality, what square observance
        Lives in a little room! Here public care
        Gags not the eyes of slumber, here fierce riot
        Ruffles not proudly in a coat of trust,
        Whilst like a pawn at chess he keeps in rank
        With kings and mighty fellows, yet indeed
        Those men that stand on tiptoe smile to see
        Him pawn his fortunes.

More   True, son.
        Nor does the wanton tongue here screw itself
        Into the ear, that like a vice drinks up
        The iron instrument.

Lady More   We are here at peace.

More   Then peace, good wife.

Lady More   For keeping still in compass (a strange point
        In time's new navigation) we have sailed
        Beyond our course.

More   Have done.

Lady More We are exiled the court.

More   Still thou harpst on that:
              'Tis sin for to deserve that banishment;
              But he that ne'er knew court, courts sweet content.

Lady More O but dear husband –

More   I will not hear thee, wife;
              The winding labyrinth of thy strange discourse
              Will ne'er have end. Sit still and, my good wife,
              Entreat thy tongue be still, or, credit me,
              Thou shalt not understand a word we speak,
              We'll talk in Latin:
              Humida vallis raros patitur fulminis ictus,
              More rest enjoys the subject meanly bred
              Than he that bears the kingdom in his head.
              Great men are still musicians, else the world lies:
              They learn low strains after the notes that rise.

Roper   Good sir, be still yourself, and but remember
              How in this general court of short-lived pleasure,
              The world, creation is the ample food
              That is digested in the maw of time.
              If man himself be subject to such ruin,
              How shall his garment then, or the loose points
              That tie respect unto his awful place,
              Avoid destruction? Most honoured father-in-law,
              The blood you have bequeathed these several hearts
              To nourish your posterity, stands firm,
              And as with joy you led us first to rise,
              So with like hearts we'll lock preferment's eyes.

More   Close them not then with tears, for that ostent
              Gives a wet signal of your discontent.
              If you will share my fortunes, comfort then:
              An hundred smiles for one sigh; what, we are men.
              Resign wet passion to these weaker eyes,
              Which proves their sex, but grants it ne'er more wise.
              Let's now survey our state: here sits my wife,
              And dear esteemèd issue, yonder stand
              My loving servants. Now the difference

'Twixt those and these. Now you shall hear my speak
Like More in melancholy. I conceive that Nature
Hath sundry metals, out of which she frames
Us mortals, each in valuation
Outprizing other. Of the finest stuff
The finest features come, the rest of earth,
Receive base fortune even before their birth.
Hence slaves have their creation, and I think
Nature provides content for the base mind:
Under the whip, the burden and the toil,
Their low-wrought bodies drudge in patience;
As for the prince, in all his sweet-gorged maw
And his rank flesh, that sinfully renews
The noon's excess in the night's dangerous surfeits;
What means or misery from our birth doth flow
Nature entitles to us, that we owe.
But we, being subject to the rack of hate,
Falling from happy life to bondage state,
Having seen better days, now know the lack
Of glory that once reared each high-fed back.
But you that in your age did ne'er view better
Challenged not fortune for your thriftless debtor.

Catesby   Sir, we have seen far better days than these.

More   I was the patron of those days, and know
Those were but painted days, only for show.
Then grieve not you to fall with him that gave them:
Generosis servis gloriosum mori.
Dear Gough, thou art my learned secretary,
You, Master Catesby, steward of my house,
The rest, like you, have had fair time to grow
In sunshine of my fortunes. But I must tell ye,
Corruption is fled hence with each man's office.
Bribes, that make open traffic 'twixt the soul
And netherland of hell, deliver up
Their guilty homage to their second lords.
Then living thus untainted, you are well:
Truth is no pilot for the land of hell.

Enter a Servant.

Servant	My lord, there are new lighted at the gate The Earls of Surrey and of Shrewsbury, And they expect you in the inner court.

More Entreat their lordships come into the hall.

Exit Servant.

Lady More O God, what news with them?

More   Why, how now wife?
They are but come to visit their old friend.

Lady More O God, I fear, I fear.

More What shouldst thou fear, fond woman?
Iustum, si fractus illabatur orbis, inpavidum ferient ruinae.
Here let me live estranged from great men's looks:
They are like golden flies on leaden hooks.

Enter the Earls, Downes with his mace, and Attendants.

Shrewsbury Good morrow, good Sir Thomas.

Kind salutations.

Surrey Good day, good madam.

More   Welcome, my good lords.
What ails your lordships look so melancholy?
O, I know you live in court, and the court diet
Is only friend to physic.

Surrey   O Sir Thomas,
Our words are now the king's, and our sad looks
The interest of your love. We are sent to you
From our mild sovereign, once more to demand
If you'll subscribe unto those articles
He sent ye th' other day. Be well advisèd,
For on mine honour, lord, grave Doctor Fisher
Bishop of Rochester, at the self same instant
Attached with you, is sent unto the Tower
For the like obstinacy; his majesty
Hath only sent you prisoner to your house.

But if you now refuse for to subscribe,
A stricter course will follow.

Lady More O, dear husband!

> *Kneeling and weeping.*

Both Daughters   Dear father!

More   See, my lords,
This partner and these subjects to my flesh
Prove rebels to my conscience. But, my good lords,
If I refuse, must I unto the Tower?

Shrewsbury You must, my lord. Here is an officer
Ready for to arrest you of high treason.

Lady More and Daughters O God, O God!

Roper   Be patient, good madam.

More Ay, Downes, is't thou? I once did save thy life,
When else by cruel riotous assault
Thou hadst been torn in pieces. Thou art reserved
To be my summoner to yond spiritual court.
Give me thy hand, good fellow, smooth thy face:
The diet that thou drinkst is spic'd with mace,
And I could ne'er abide it: 'twill not digest,
'Twill lie too heavily, man, on my weak breast.

Shrewsbury Be brief, my lord, for we are limited
Unto an hour.

More   Unto an hour? 'Tis well,
The bell soon shall toll my knell.

Lady More Dear loving husband, if you respect not me,
Yet think upon your daughters.

> *Kneeling.*

More Wife, stand up. I have bethought me,
And I'll now satisfy the king's good pleasure.

> *Pondering to himself.*

Both Daughters O happy alteration.

Shrewsbury Come then, subscribe, my lord.

Surrey   I am right glad
          Of this your fair conversion.

More   O, pardon me,
          I will subscribe to go unto the Tower
          With all submissive willingness, and thereto add
          My bones to strengthen the foundation
          Of Julius Caesar's palace. Now, my lord,
          I'll satisfy the king even with my blood;
          Nor will I wrong your patience. Friend, do thine
                                                    office.

Downes   Sir Thomas More, Lord Chancellor of England,
          I arrest you in the king's name of high treason.

More   Gramercies, friend.
          To a great prison, to discharge the strife
          Commenced 'twixt conscience and my frailer life,
          More now must march. Chelsea, adieu, adieu,
          Strange farewell, thou shalt ne'er more see More true,
          For I shall ne'er see thee more. Servants, farewell.
          Wife, mar not thine indifferent face, be wise:
          More's widow's husband, he must make thee rise.
          Daughters what's here, what's here?
          Mine eye had almost parted with a tear.
          Dear son, possess my virtue, that I ne'er gave.
          Grave More thus lightly walks to a quick grave.

Roper   *Curae leves loquuntur, ingentes stupent.*

More   You that way in, mind you my course in prayer:
          By water I to prison, to heaven through air.

                                        Exeunt.

ACT FIVE

SCENE ONE

Enter the Warders of the Tower, with halberds.

First Warder   Ho, make a guard there.

Second Warder   Master Lieutenant gives a straight command
        The people be avoided from the bridge.

Third Warder   From whence is he committed, who can tell?

First Warder   From Durham House, I hear.

Second Warder   The guard were waiting there an hour ago.

Third Warder   If he stay long, he'll not get near the wharf,
        There's such a crowd of boats upon the Thames.

Second Warder   Well, be it spoken without offence to any,
        A wiser or more virtuous gentleman
        Was never bred in England.

Third Warder   I think, the poor will bury him in tears.
        I never heard a man, since I was born
        So generally bewailed of everyone.

Enter a Poor Woman.

        What means this woman? – Whither dost thou press?

First Warder   This woman will be trod to death anon.

Second Warder   What mak'st thou here?

Woman   To speak with that good man, Sir Thomas More.

Second Warder   To speak with him? He's not Lord Chancellor.

Woman   The more's the pity, sir, if it pleased God.

Second Warder   Therefore, if thou hast a petition to deliver,
        Thou mayst keep it now, for anything I know.

Woman   I am a poor woman, and have had (God knows)
          A suit this two year in the Chancery;
          And he hath all the evidence I have
          Which should I lose, I am utterly undone.

Second Warder   Faith, and I fear thou'lt hardly come by 'em now;
          I am sorry for thee even with all my heart.

          Enter the Lords of Shrewsbury and Surrey
          with Sir Thomas More, and Attendants,
          and enter Lieutenant and Gentleman Porter.

          Woman, stand back, you must avoid this place,
          The lords must pass this way into the Tower.

More   I thank your lordships for your pains thus far
          To my strong house.

Woman   Now, good Sir Thomas More, for Christ's dear sake,
          Deliver me my writings back again
          That do concern my title.

More   What, my old client, are thou got hither too?
          Poor silly wretch, I must confess indeed
          I had such writings as concern thee near,
          But the king has ta'en the matter into his own hand:
          He has all I had; then, woman, sue to him,
          I cannot help thee, thou must bear with me.

Woman   Ah, gentle heart, my soul for thee is sad,
          Farewell the best friend that the poor e'er had.
                                        Exit Woman.

Gentleman Porter   Before you enter through the Tower gate,
          Your upper garment, sir, belongs to me.

More   Sir, you shall have it, there it is.
                                        He gives him his cap.

Gentleman Porter   The upmost on your back, sir, you mistake me.

More   Sir, now I understand ye very well,
          But that you name my back;
          Sure else my cap had been the uppermost.

Shrewsbury	Farewell, kind lord, God send us merry meeting.
More	Amen, my lord.
Surrey	Farewell, dear friend, I hope your safe return.
More	My lord, and my dear fellow in the Muses,
	Farewell, farewell, most noble poet.
Lieutenant	Adieu, most honoured lords.

Exeunt Lords.

More	Fair prison, welcome. Yet methinks,

For thy fair building 'tis too foul a name.
Many a guilty soul, and many an innocent,
Have breathed their farewell to thy hollow rooms.
I oft have entered into thee this way,
Yet, I thank God, ne'er with a clearer conscience
Than at this hour.
This is my comfort yet: how hard soe'er
My lodging prove, the cry of the poor suitor,
Fatherless orphan, or distressèd widow
Shall not disturb me in my quiet sleep.
On then, a God's name, to our close abode.
God is as strong here as he is abroad.

Exeunt.

SCENE TWO

Enter Butler, Porter, and Horsekeeper several ways.

Butler	Robin brewer, how now man? What cheer, what cheer?
Brewer	Faith, Ned butler, sick of thy disease; and these our other fellows here, Rafe horsekeeper and Giles porter, sad, sad; they say my lord goes to his trial today.
Horsekeeper	To it, man? Why, he is now at it, God send him well to speed.

Porter	Amen. Even as I wish to mine own soul, so speed it with my honourable lord and master Sir Thomas More.
Butler	I cannot tell, I have nothing to do with matters above my capacity, but as God judge me, if I might speak my mind, I think there lives not a more harmless gentleman in the universal world.
Brewer	Nor a wiser, nor a merrier, nor an honester. Go to, I'll put that in upon mine own knowledge.
Porter	Nay, and ye bate him his due of his housekeeping, hang ye all. Ye have many Lord Chancellors comes in debt at the year's end, and for very housekeeping.
Horsekeeper	Well, he was too good a lord for us, and therefore, I fear, God himself will take him. But I'll be hanged, if ever I have such another service.
Brewer	Soft, man, we are not discharged yet. My lord may come home again and all will be well.
Butler	I much mistrust it: when they go to 'raigning once, there's ever foul weather for a great while after. But soft, here comes Master Gough and Master Catesby: now we shall hear more.

Enter Gough and Catesby with a paper.

Horsekeeper	Before God, they are very sad, I doubt my lord is condemned.
Porter	God bless his soul, and a fig then for all worldly condemnation.
Gough	Well said, Giles porter, I commend thee for it, 'Twas spoken like a well affected servant Of him that was a kind lord to us all.
Catesby	Which now no more he shall be, for, dear fellows, Now we are masterless, though he may live So long as please the king. But law hath made him A dead man to the world, and given the axe his head, But his sweet soul to live among the saints.

Gough   Let us entreat ye to go call together
             The rest of your sad fellows (by the roll
             Y'are just seven score), and tell them what ye hear
             A virtuous honourable lord hath done
             Even for the meanest follower that he had.
             This writing found my lady in his study
             This instant morning, wherein is set down
             Each servant's name, according to his place
             And office in the house. On every man
             He frankly hath bestowen twenty nobles,
             The best and worst together, all alike,
             Which Master Catesby here forth will pay ye.

Catesby   Take it as it is meant, a kind remembrance
             Of a far kinder lord, with whose sad fall
             He gives up house, and farewell to us all.
             Thus the fair spreading oak falls not alone,
             But all the neighbour plants and under-trees
             Are crushed down with his weight. No more of this,
             Come and receive your due, and after go
             Fellow-like hence, co-partners of one woe.

                                                    Exeunt.

SCENE THREE

Enter Sir Thomas More, the Lieutenant,
and a Servant attending, as in his chamber in the Tower.

More   Master Lieutenant, is the warrant come?
             If it be so, a God's name let us know it.

Lieutenant   My lord, it is.

More   'Tis welcome, sir, to me,
             With all my heart. His blessed will be done.

Lieutenant   Your wisdom, sir, hath been so well approved,
             And your fair patience in imprisonment
             Hath ever shown such constancy of mind
             And Christian resolution in all troubles,
             As warrants us you are not unprepared.

More	No, Master Lieutenant; ·
	I thank my God, I have peace of conscience,
	Though the world and I are at a little odds.
	But we'll be even now, I hope, ere long.
	When is the execution of your warrant?
Lieutenant	Tomorrow morning.
More	So, sir, I thank ye.
	I have not lived so ill I fear to die.
	Master Lieutenant,
	I have had a sore fit of the stone tonight,
	But the king hath sent me such a rare receipt,
	I thank him, as I shall not need to fear it much.
Lieutenant	In life and death still merry Sir Thomas More.
More	Sirrah fellow, reach me the urinal.

He gives it him.

	Ha, let me see. There's gravel in the water
	(And yet I see no grave danger in that):
	The man were likely to live long enough,
	So pleased the king. Here, fellow, take it.
Servant	Shall I go with it to the doctor, sir?
More	No, save thy labour, we'll cozen him of a fee.
	Thou shalt see me take a dram tomorrow morning,
	Shall cure the stone I warrant, doubt it not.
	Master Lieutenant, what news of my Lord of
	Rochester?
Lieutenant	Yesterday morning was he put to death.
More	The peace of soul sleep with him.
	He was a learned and a reverend prelate,
	And a rich man, believe me.
Lieutenant	If he were rich, what is Sir Thomas More,
	That all this while hath been lord chancellor?
More	Say ye so, master lieutenant? What do you think
	A man that with my time had held my place
	Might purchase?

Lieutenant	Perhaps, my lord, two thousand pound a year.
More	Master lieutenant, I protest to you,
	I never had the means in all my life
	To purchase one poor hundred pound a year.
	I think I am the poorest chancellor
	That ever was in England, though I could wish,
	For credit of the place, that my estate were better.
Lieutenant	It's very strange.
More	It will be found as true.
	I think, sir, that with most part of my coin
	I have purchased as strange commodities
	As ever you heard tell of in your life.
Lieutenant	Commodities, my lord?
	Might I, without offence, enquire of them?
More	Crutches, master lieutenant, and bare cloaks.
	For halting soldiers, and poor needy scholars,
	Have had my gettings in the chancery.
	To think but what a cheat the crown shall have
	By my attainder!
	I prithee, if thou beest a gentleman,
	Get but a copy of my inventory.
	That part of poet that was given me
	Made me a very unthrift.
	For this is the disease attends us all:
	Poets were never thrifty, never shall.

Enter Lady More mourning, Daughters, Master Roper.

Lieutenant	O, noble More. –
	My lord, your wife, your son-in-law, and daughters.
More	Son Roper, welcome; welcome, wife and girls.
	Why do you weep? Because I live at ease?
	Did you not see, when I was chancellor,
	I was so clogged with suitors every hour,
	I could not sleep, nor dine, nor sup in quiet?
	Here's none of this; here I can sit and talk
	With my honest keeper half a day together,
	Laugh and be merry. Why, then, should you weep?

Roper	These tears, my lord, for this your long restraint Hope had dried up, with comfort that we yet, Although imprisoned, might have had your life.
More	To live in prison, what a life were that? The king (I thank him) loves me more than so. Tomorrow I shall be at liberty To go even whither I can, After I have dispatched my business.
Lady More	Ah, husband, husband, yet submit yourself, Have care of your poor wife and children.
More	Wife, so I have, and I do leave you all To His protection hath the power to keep you Safer than I can, The father of the widow and the orphan.
Roper	The world, my lord, hath ever held you wise, And 't shall be no distaste unto your wisdom, To yield to the opinion of the state.
More	I have deceived myself, I must acknowledge; And, as you say, son Roper, to confess the same, It will be no disparagement at all.
Lady More	His highness shall be certified thereof, immediately.

Offering to depart.

More	Nay, hear me, wife, first let me tell ye how. I thought to have had a barber for my beard, Now I remember that were labour lost, The headsman now shall cut off head and all.
Roper's Wife	Father, his majesty upon your meek submission Will yet, they say, receive you to his grace In as great credit as you were before.
More	. . . Faith, my Lord the king Has appointed me to do a little business. If that were past, my girl, thou then shouldst see What I would say to him about that matter. But I shall be so busy until then, I shall not tend it.

Daughter   Ah, my dear father.

Lady More   Dear lord and husband.

More   Be comforted, good wife, to live and love my children,
                For with thee leave I all my care of them.
                Son Roper, for my sake that have loved thee well,
                And for her virtue's sake, cherish my child.
                Girl, be not proud, but of thy husband's love;
                Ever retain thy virtuous modesty.
                That modesty is such a comely garment
                As it is never out of fashion, sits as fair
                Upon the meaner woman as the empress.
                No stuff that gold can buy is half so rich,
                Nor ornament that so becomes a woman.
                Live all, and love together, and thereby
                You give your father a rich obsequy.

Both Daughters   Your blessing, dear father.

More   I must be gone, God bless you,
                To talk with God, who now doth call.

Lady More   Ah, my dear husband.

More   Sweet wife, good night, good night:
                God send us all his everlasting light.

Roper   I think, before this hour,
                More heavy hearts ne'er parted in the Tower.

                                                    Exeunt.

SCENE FOUR

*Enter the Sheriffs of London and their Officers at one door,
the Warders with their halberds at another.*

Second Sheriff   Officers, what time of day is't?

Officer   Almost eight o'clock.

Second Sheriff   We must make haste then, lest we stay too long.

Second Warder   Good morrow, master shrieves of London;
                                                master lieutenant
             Wills ye repair to the limits of the Tower,
             There to receive your prisoner.

First Sheriff Go back, and tell his worship we are ready.

Second Sheriff   Go bid the officers make clear the way,
             There may be passage for the prisoner.

              Enter Lieutenant and his Guard, with More.

More   Yet, God be thanked, here's a fair day toward,
             To take our journey in. Master Lieutenant,
             It were fair walking on the Tower leads.

Lieutenant And so it might have liked my sovereign lord,
             I would to God you might have walked there still.

                                                He weeps.

More   Sir, we are walking to a better place.
             O sir, your kind and loving tears
             Are like sweet odours to embalm your friend.
             Thank your good lady, since I was your guest
             She has made me a very wanton, in good sooth.

Lieutenant O, I had hoped we should not yet have parted.

More   But I must leave ye for a little while.
             Within an hour or two you may look for me,
             But there will be so many come to see me
             That I shall be so proud I will not speak.
             And sure my memory is grown so ill
             I fear I shall forget my head behind me.

Lieutenant God and his blessed angels be about ye.
             Here, master shrieves, receive your prisoner.

More   Good morrow, master shrieves of London, to ye both.
             I thank ye that ye will vouchsafe to meet me.
             I see by this you have not quite forgot
             That I was in times past as you are now:
             A sheriff of London.

Second Sheriff   Sir, then you know our duty doth require it.

More   I know it well, sir, else I would have been glad
                You might have saved a labour at this time.
                Ah, master sheriff, you and I have been of old
                acquaintance: you were a patient auditor of mine
                when I read the divinity lecture at St. Lawrence's.

Second Sheriff   Sir Thomas More, I have heard you oft,
                As many other did, to our great comfort.

More   Pray God you may so now, with all my heart.
                And, as I call to mind,
                When I studied the law in Lincoln's Inn,
                I was of counsel with ye in a cause.

Second Sheriff   I was about to say so, good Sir Thomas.

More   O, is this the place?
                I promise ye, it is a goodly scaffold.
                In sooth, I am come about a headless errand,
                For I have not much to say, now I am here.
                Well, let's ascend, a God's name.
                In troth, methinks, your stair is somewhat weak:
                I prithee, honest friend, lend me thy hand
                To help me up. As for my coming down,
                Let me alone, I'll look to that myself.

                     As he is going up the stairs,
                enters the Earls of Surrey and Shrewsbury.

                My Lords of Surrey and Shrewsbury, give me your
                hands. Yet before we part. Ye see, though it pleaseth
                the king to raise me thus high, yet I am not proud,
                for the higher I mount, the better I can see my
                friends about me. I am now on a far voyage, and this
                strange wooden horse must bear me thither; yet I
                perceive by your looks you like my bargain so ill,
                that there's not one of ye all dare venture with me.
                Truly, here's a most sweet gallery, (*Walking*) I like the
                air of it better than my garden at Chelsea. By your
                patience, good people, that have pressed thus into
                my bedchamber, if you'll not trouble me, I'll take a
                sound sleep here.

Shrewsbury	My lord, 'twere good you'd publish to the world Your great offence unto his majesty.
More	My lord, I'll bequeath this legacy to the hangman, (*Gives him his gown*) and do it instantly. I confess his majesty hath been ever good to me, and my offence to his highness makes me of a state pleader a stage player (though I am old, and have a bad voice), to act this last scene of my tragedy. I'll send him for my trespass a reverend head, somewhat bald, for it is not requisite any head should stand covered to so high majesty. If that content him not, because I think my body will then do me small pleasure, let him but bury it, and take it.
Surrey	My lord, my lord, hold conference with your soul: You see, my lord, the time of life is short.
More	I see it, my good lord; I dispatched that business the last night. I come hither only to be let blood: my doctor here tells me it is good for the headache.
Hangman	I beseech thee, my lord, forgive me.
More	Forgive thee, honest fellow? Why?
Hangman	For your death, my lord.
More	O, my death? I had rather it were in thy power to forgive me, for thou hast the sharpest action against me; the law, my honest friend, lies in thy hands now. Here's thy fee (*His purse*); and, my good fellow, let my suit be dispatched presently; for 'tis all one pain, to die a lingering death and to live in the continual mill of a lawsuit. But I can tell thee, my neck is so short, that, if thou shouldst behead an hundred noblemen like myself, thou wouldst ne'er get credit by it. Therefore look ye, sir, do it handsomely, or, of my word, thou shalt never deal with me hereafter.
Hangman	I'll take an order for that, my lord.
More	One thing more, take heed thou cutst not off my beard. O, I forgot, execution passed upon that last night, and the body of it lies buried in the Tower. –

Stay; is't not possible to make a scape from all this
strong guard? It is.
There is a thing within me, that will raise
And elevate my better part 'bove sight
Of these same weaker eyes. And, master shrieves,
For all this troop of steel that tends my death,
I shall break from you, and fly up to heaven.
Let's seek the means for this.

Hangman   My lord, I pray ye put off your doublet.

More   Speak not so coldly to me, I am hoarse already,
I would be loath, good fellow, to take more.
Point me the block, I ne'er was here before.

Hangman   To the east side, my lord.

More   Then to the east
We go to sigh, that o'er, to sleep in rest.
Here More forsakes all mirth, good reason why:
The fool of flesh must with her frail life die.
No eye salute my trunk with a sad tear;
Our birth to heaven should be thus: void of fear.

Exit with Hangman.

Surrey   A very learned worthy gentleman
Seals error with his blood. Come, we'll to court.
Let's sadly hence to perfect unknown fates,
Whilst he tends progress to the state of states.

Exeunt.

FINIS

A Nick Hern Book

This edition of *Sir Thomas More*
first published in Great Britain in 2005
as a paperback original by
Nick Hern Books Limited
14 Larden Road, London W3 7ST
in association with the
Royal Shakespeare Company

Copyright in this edition
© 2005 Royal Shakespeare Company

Copyright in the introductory material © 2005
Gregory Doran, Ann Pasternak Slater, Martin White

Cover design by Andy Williams, RSC Graphics

Typeset by Country Setting, Kingsdown, Kent CT14 8ES
Printed and bound in Great Britain
by Bookmarque, Croydon, Surrey

A CIP catalogue record for this book is available from
the British Library

ISBN 1 85459 859 7